A
P A U S E
in
the
RAIN

To Rebekah,
in case you run out
of reading material!
Joy Greenberg 7-1-09

A PAUSE in the RAIN

A Memoir

Joy Greenberg

For Maceo, Gian and Greg:
That you may experience the love which created you
and your father, whose spirit lives forever in you

CONTENTS

ACKNOWLEDGMENTS

I would not have attempted the task of writing a story about Chuck Greenberg and Shadowfax without the collaboration of the band members. Phil, Stu and G.E—the original 'Faxmen—all contributed considerably to this effort, and for that I am grateful. Among the many others who provided generous inspiration, encouragement, editing, and memories are Jeannette Kraar, Suzin Kortokrax, Janice Stein, Warren Flaschen, Dallas Westerfield, Steven Lowy, Armen Chakmakian, Stevo, Susan Harris, Jeff Paris, Bill Johnston, Rob Mayer, Mary Tartaglione, and my indomitable faculty advisors: Paul Eggers, Susann Cokal and Steven Marx.

Thank you all.

FOREWORD

Chuck Greenberg had more music in him than anyone I ever met. I don't mean just notes, I mean notes that mattered. You could call Chuck in for a session on a piece he'd never heard and he'd simply start playing and break your heart. This wasn't just a guy playing music. It was a guy who was so connected to music that every note at least touched his soul on the way out and it usually went a lot deeper than that. Some of the finest melodies I've heard in a life of being surrounded by brilliant musicians came from Chuck Greenberg. He graced my music along with a host of others while tending to the brilliant band Shadowfax. And if it wasn't enough that he had all this talent, he was also a man who lived about twice as large as most. This was not someone who was sleepwalking though life. It seemed he needed to feel everything there was, good and bad. What he chose to leave us with, though, was all good. I will miss the man, but be grateful we recorded so much of the musician.

William Ackerman

PREFACE

...And this is what every great artist comes to learn en route: that the process in which he is involved has to do with another dimension of life, that by identifying himself with this process he augments life. In this view of things he is permanently removed—and protected—from that insidious death which seems to triumph all about him. He divines that the great secret will never be apprehended but incorporated in his very substance. He has to make himself a part of the mystery, live in it as well as with it. Through art...one finally establishes contact with reality; that is the great discovery.

Henry Miller, *On Writing*

Because my husband, Chuck Greenberg, was an artist who happened to be fond of Henry Miller's work, a friend printed the above words onto a poster and gave it to me when Chuck died in 1995. Miller's quotation so impressed me that I framed the poster and hung it in my home. Part of its fascination derived from the fact that I wasn't very certain about Miller's intended meaning.

Years later, while taking a writing course, I became acquainted with Charles Taylor's notion of modern identity as detailed in his book *Sources of the Self.* I acquired a new appreciation for Miller's words, connected to the realization that he speaks of the establishment of self-identity, the "sense of ourselves as beings with inner depths." It is this notion of identity that underlies all "beingness," defining who we are and what we hope to be, helping us contextualize our lives in a world that's become increasingly complex. It is a notion of particular significance to artists, for it is through creativity that one's "self" is affirmed. Art as a manifestation of the self is the ultimate affirmation of life—of immortality. Indeed, the need to express one's position in regard to the universe is an immemorial urge. In Chuck's case, his musical artistry allowed him, essentially, to live forever.

I believe that this perpetual quest for immortality is what drives all artists. Integral to this quest is self discovery, which often occurs as epiphany—a transcendental experience. And with epiphany comes understanding which, hopefully, adds meaning to one's life. It is this "aspiration for meaning and substance in one's life [that] has obvious affinities with... aspirations...to immortality," explains Taylor. Thus Miller's "contact with reality," which artists establish through creativity, is, in fact, the fulfillment of this quest for immortality. Chuck's singularity was that his contact with reality—his immortality—came through his music. Even now, despite his many years of absence from our lives, all of us who knew Chuck—if only through his music—continue to receive affirmation of his immortality. For example, fan Dan Cain wrote:

> Chuck's music was very emotional to me. Like life itself. Within the music's resonance and tonal qualities I seem to sense the essence of life and death, joy and sorrow, love and pain and the secrets of creation for us all. Visual and emotional imagery wells up from within, striking chords of feelings and worldly experiences that all humans are familiar with from life. I think his music should live on forever.

But Chuck's immortality stems not only from his artistry, but from his entire persona and interpersonal relationships—he was someone many people, myself included, called their "best friend." It is because of Chuck that I have the temerity to pursue my own artistry. And being an artist requires much temerity: who but the most audacious of souls would dare aspire to immortality?

Chuck in 1972, courtesy of Jeff Paris

* * *

However circuitous the route leading to my metamorphosis into a writer, and despite the gaps and lapses that exist in terms of my productivity in this realm, one thing is certain: I have always wanted to be an artist, if not a writer. It is an aspiration that finds me diving inward to the depths—the very essence, I suppose, of my being—following the paths of the many writers before me who looked within and reported their findings. It is a process fraught with discoveries—some of which might be better left alone to dwell unexposed in the obscure shadows of my psyche. As Henry Thoreau wrote: "It is easier to sail many thousand miles through cold and storm and cannibals, in a government ship, with five hundred men and boys to assist one, than it is to explore the private sea, the Atlantic and Pacific Ocean of one's being alone." Thoreau's metaphor is apt, for writing is a task not unlike diving into deep water without knowing what obstacles might lurk beneath the surface, waiting to snag and rend the mind and body. But if the water is clear, the artist finds her life illumined in ways not otherwise possible. It is this aptitude for risk, this obsession with discovery, which truly defined Chuck as an artist and defines me as well.

When Chuck died, I began writing about him and his life as a musician and leader of the Grammy Award-winning band Shadowfax. It was something I had long considered, and it finally seemed to be the right time. Through writing and the retelling of his tale, I was hoping for catharsis and closure—a sort of working through the grief. I was also trying to memorialize him—to make sure he would not be forgotten, especially by our three sons, who were able to enjoy their father for so few years. In a way, I felt driven by the need to "make sense of [Chuck's] life as a story" which, as Charles Taylor says, is "not an optional extra...our lives exist...in this space of questions, which only a coherent narrative can answer."

To me, Chuck's was a compelling story that appeared to have all the classic elements, complete with a universal theme of "man rising against adversity," despite his humble middle class origins. Indeed, it seemed the stuff from which myths evolve. However, what I discovered in the process of recreating Chuck's story was that I could not write about him without writing about myself. And therein lay the rub: Doing the job right meant exposing my Self in ways that I wasn't sure were prudent. Doubts surfaced telling me why this wasn't such a good idea: What if someone's privacy was compromised? What if *my* privacy was compromised? What might my sons think? And, finally, *who am I*, anyway, why am I doing this, and why am I here?

Despite these concerns, I forged ahead, writing, revising, going through my photography archives, interviewing old friends, and, of course, crying. God, did I ever cry! There seemed to be no end to the tears. I wept at least a thousand teardrops—to borrow a song title from Chuck—while writing and remembering, remembering and suffering. But it was a cleansing, cathartic suffering, for through it all, the agonizing grief seemed to ease.

Or maybe I just became more accustomed to the suffering, like an old shirt that is worn so often it becomes a second skin. Perhaps we Westerners have it all wrong about suffering. Rather than assiduously avoiding it, we might do better embracing it. I must become this agonizing grief, make it mine. I must accept grief for what it is: yet another of life's many affirmations. I suffer, therefore I exist. In suffering, I know that I'm alive and in touch with the essence of my being. I am in "contact with reality."

Despite the suffering, I am thankful to have known Chuck—*and* Shadowfax. As Sound Guy Stevo said whenever he introduced the band onstage, "This is the most unusual group of guys ever to call themselves a band." In my never-ending quest for the weird and bizarre, Shadowfax has not disappointed me.

Of course, my perspective is that of an insider, and therefore necessarily subjective. But, with the luxury of hindsight, I have attempted to put together The Shadowfax Story—that is, the one I experienced after meeting founding member Chuck Greenberg. This is not intended to be "definitive" or the "whole" story by any means. It is simply *my* story, for that is the one I best know and am able to recount. Hopefully, my perspective transcends the average music biography and enters the realm of "creative nonfiction," wherein "memory and imagination [become] the same human property, known by different names," as Tony Earley says in his remarkable memoir *Somehow Form a Family*. Isn't that, after all, what all art is about?

What writers like Taylor and Earley have done is help me to define my identity. Lynne Tillman says that "writing gives me an identity, a thing to be in the world." But my writing, like anyone else's, does not take place in a vacuum. It takes place in a community—ostensibly one that is created by those who read my writing. My reading audience is therefore my community. The challenge is not to allow my agenda, my "issues," to *become* my identity. As James Baldwin writes, his father's "inability to establish contact with other people had always marked him" and haunted him for the rest of his life. For Baldwin's father, bitterness and hatred *became* his identity, at the expense of relating effectively to his community. Thus, although he was a gifted preacher, few people listened to him. In other words, a balance must be created between our individual identities and our communities if we are to be self-actualized humans.

First Shadowfax publicity still, 1982: Jared Stewart, Jamii Szmadzinski,
Phil Maggini, G.E. Stinson, Chuck Greenberg and Stu Nevitt, [l-r];
courtesy of Frank B. Denham/Windham Hill Records

Balancing identity with community is further exacerbated by the issue of religion. Just as Salman Rushdie's patriarch, Dr. Adam Aziz, in *Midnight's Children* "loses his faith and is left with 'a hole inside him,'" like Rushdie, "I, too, possess that same God-shaped hole. Unable to accept the unarguable absolutes of religion, I have tried to fill up the hole with literature." In some ways, *writing* has become my religion; readers are my congregation, my community.

xviii

The commitment I make to my religion and congregation is that although my writing may challenge the complacent and resist structures and institutions that serve the powerful, it comes from my heart, just as Chuck's art—his music—came from *his* heart. Chuck's music was *his* contact with reality—his truth. Writing is *mine*.

The significance of this "contact with reality" is a message reiterated by Italo Calvino in *Invisible Cities*, in which the narrator tells us that cities, like people, are not defined by *things*, but by *details*. Reality is not the objects we surround ourselves with but the abstract ideas and memories we have combined with the choices we make. Just as Calvino's final city, Berenice, befits its name's translation as a "bringer of victory" despite the fact that it is "unjust," so is there hope for all people who have the opportunity to keep changing and redefining their lives and selves. As Polo tells Khan:

> The inferno of the living is not something that will be…it is where we live every day [but] there are two ways to escape suffering it. The first is [to] accept the inferno…The second is [to] seek and learn to recognize who and what, in the midst of the inferno, are not inferno, then make them endure…

Through *A Pause in the Rain* I am able to acknowledge those who are not "inferno" and "make them endure." By writing about Chuck, our children, and myself, I have helped us endure. I have contacted reality.

ANOTHER COUNTRY
TROPICO BLUE
STREETNOISE
NIGHT PASSAGE
ARIKI
CASTANEDA'S BOOGIE
① PAUSE IN RAIN / Include me out
FOUNDWIND ③ out
① ZIMBABWE / HEY your HATS!
SHAMAN SONG
SHADOWDANCE
IMAGINARY ISLAND
NEITHER/NOR
BROWN RICE

TWO-HEADED ALARM
CLOCK

Shadowfax Set List [Chuck's handwriting], 1995

I

SOMETHING
ABOUT
HIS
EYES

With the gleam of a Christmas elf in his eye, he
drew me into the magic of his musical dreams.
                                        Russ Davis

C huck blew into my life much like the Santa Anas that accompanied him on a November day in 1980. Despite the raging wind outside, a forties-style fedora perched upon his strawberry blond curls. It was a color—magenta—my mother had once told me redheads should never wear, but on Chuck it was enchanting. His eyes twinkled behind oversized horn-rims and a crooked grin fought with a trim beard for attention. Sizing him up, I noticed his black shirt unbuttoned at the neck so that just a bit of reddish chest hair was exposed. Although he was attempting to be suave, I could tell that—like me—he was nervous, but Chuck immediately put me at ease. Uncorking the red wine he'd brought and lighting a cigarette, he began asking about the '55 Chevy Bel Air sedan he'd seen parked in the carport out front.

"That was my grandmother's in Dallas, and when she died two years ago, my mother drove it out to L.A.," I said, pleased that he'd noticed my prized heirloom. "After my mother died last May, I decided to keep it."

"Cool." Chuck exhaled a plume of smoke. "Not that your mother died," he hastened to add, "but I've got a '65 Bel Air coupe. Maybe we can park them side by side and mate them," he deadpanned. The image of baby Bel Airs popping out of car trunks cracked me up and I momentarily forgot about the cigarette smoking, a habit I disdained.

Chuck "playing" a tripod, 1982,
courtesy of Frank B. Denman/Windham Hill Records

"Speaking of mating," I said, noting his reddish hair, "if we ever have kids, they'll all be redheads." It was one detail I'd remembered from high school biology: Red-haired offspring were the only possible results from red-haired parents. I immediately regretted this comment, thinking he might take it as an invitation to sex, which, of course, he did.

"Are you telling me you've genetically selected me for breeding purposes?" he shot back, apparently unfazed by my forwardness. I laughed and turned bright red, wondering when I'd learn not to blurt the first thing that came into my head.

"I don't know," I said. "It depends on how well we get along..."

"Let's find out right now," he said, without missing a beat. He grabbed my hand and the bottle of wine. "Where's your room?"

"That isn't exactly what I had in mind," I said, but I was beginning to realize that Chuck was not someone who could be dissuaded easily. There was something alluring about this curly-haired guy with the sparkling blue eyes. "Upstairs," I said, pointing at the spiral staircase by the front door.

* * *

Our blind date had been set up as a spontaneous end to what began as a windy but otherwise routine Saturday. The Santa Ana had picked up even more by the time I returned from my late-afternoon skate. Sand and trash now littered the Venice Beach bike path, creating an obstacle course through which I had to jump and pick my way. Sweating from the combination of exertion and intense heat, I finally managed to clomp my way back to the beachfront apartment I shared, to find my roommate and his new girlfriend relaxing by the fireplace. As if it weren't hot enough already, they had a fire going. After all, Ted was from the East Coast, where hearthside fires were synonymous with winter, which it technically now was. He had just finished skating for the day too, and invited me to sip some wine with him while contemplating various possibilities for the evening's entertainment. With him was Tiffany, the latest addition to his stable of girlfriends: a long-legged, blonde nurse he'd met at Santa Monica Hospital, where he was finishing his family practice residency. I downed a glass of water, plopped onto the sofa, removed my skates and began cleaning the sand out of the ball bearings.

Tiffany lit a joint and passed it to me, asking if I had a date for the evening. I confessed that I hadn't. "Actually, I just broke up with a guy in New York," I said, between tokes. "I'm still licking my wounds. I don't think I'm in the market for a boyfriend right now."

"I know lots of guys," she said, throwing a sideways glance at Ted. "Let me know when you're interested in meeting them." It occurred to me that if I *were* to be looking, Tiffany could probably provide valuable assistance, for she seemed to have a handle on this issue. In fact, as she continued speaking, she revealed herself to be an expert. In a matter-of-fact tone, Tiffany allowed that she burned through men the way some people spend money, without the slightest heed to the consequences of their consumerism.

I took the bait. "Okay, you've aroused my curiosity. So what's available?"

Tiffany scratched her head and considered this question. After pausing for some moments, her eyes brightened and she ventured, "Well, there's always Chuck..." Her voice trailed off with what I perceived to be an element of uncertainty.

"So tell me about Chuck," I coaxed.

"Actually, I can't say enough nice things about Chuck," she said, regaining her composure.

My interest was piqued.

"He loves women and he's very nice to his girlfriends," she continued.

"How do you know?" I said.

"He's my roommate," she replied. "I know *everything* about him. Plus, he's got a great sense of humor."

We were beginning to get somewhere, I thought. Laughter was high on my agenda.

"But I should tell you a few more things," Tiffany said. Uh-oh, here it comes, I thought. I crossed my fingers that Chuck wasn't a stalker or serial psychopath. "Number One," she continued. "He's got red hair—kinda like yours, in fact, only curlier."

"Oh," I said, the enthusiasm draining from my voice. I'd always thought that redheaded guys were dorky-looking—something to do with invisible eyelashes—but I was willing to reserve judgment until the initial sighting.

"Number Two: He's Jewish."

"Oh, no," I said before I could catch myself. "I just broke up with a Jewish boyfriend," I added quickly. "Maybe I need a change of pace."

"Chuck's from Chicago," Tiffany said. "You know," she advised with a hint of conspiracy, "the farther away from New York a Jew gets, the less fucked up he is." Before I could question her scientific methodology, she went on.

"Number Three: He smokes cigarettes." She already knew how I felt about that. "But he's trying to stop," she said, as if feeling the need to bolster his character. "By the way," she added, almost as an afterthought, "Do you like music? Because he's a musician."

Now, this fact was tantalizing. Like most thirty-one-year-olds, I was a devoted music fan, but fantasizing about being a rock star was the closest I'd ever come to one, aside from a stint in San Francisco as a Grateful Deadhead during my early twenties. So when Tiffany mentioned the magic word "musician," my attention was snagged. Visions of glitzy parties and beautiful people cavorted in my head, not to mention drugs. Weren't musicians notorious drug users? Still, I was wary. After all, what was any self-respecting musician doing home alone on a Saturday night? And the name "Chuck" didn't sound like a typical rock star name. "Charlie," maybe, but not "Chuck." Perhaps I needed to extract more information.

"So, what kind of music does he play?" I asked.

"Woodwinds—you know, flutes and saxes," she said. "And this really trippy wind synth called a lyricon."

While winds were not as glamorous as guitars, my father had played a silver Haynes and my last name, after all, was Horner. And, there did seem to be something karmic about a wind-player. Maybe this Santa Ana wind was a good omen, despite all the rumors about positive ions.

"Well," I said, trying not to sound too eager, "see if you can get him over here, but be discreet." I had my pride, after all.

With that, Tiffany got on the phone with Chuck, gushing, "Come over right now. I've got a hot one for you."

So much for "discreet."

* * *

Next thing I knew, Chuck was leading me up to my room, where we settled onto my king-sized waterbed. I wasn't accustomed to inviting guys into my bedroom on the first date. However, there really was something appealing about Chuck that made him seem different from all the other guys I'd known. He seemed like a man with a plan.

No sooner had we sat down than we could hear thuds and groans emanating from Ted's room, directly below mine. I recognized the source at the same instant I grasped it was not the soundtrack I had in mind for my blind date with Chuck. I considered blaming the noise on the wind before deciding Chuck was too savvy to believe this.

"Don't worry," I said, "I know it sounds like they're killing each other, but I never see any blood or bruises afterward. They're just having a little fun, if you know what I mean, heh heh." I tried to sound blasé, as if earthshaking thumps accompanied by a rhythmic humph... humph... humph happened all the time.

6

"I know all about Tiffany and her brand of 'fun,'" Chuck said, rolling his eyes. I noticed again their sparkling, elfin quality. "Must've been a good score at the hospital," he said, referring to the med samples that both Ted and Tiffany brought home from time to time.

"What's the deal with you and Tiffany, anyway? She said you're 'just roommates.' Is that true?"

"Absolutely," he said. "When my girlfriend split three months ago, I needed someone to help pay the rent. Turns out Tiffany needed a place after she got kicked out of the bass player's house for cheating on him. So I let her move in with me. Big mistake. The bass player's always asking me what she's up to, which puts me in the middle, 'cause she brings home a different guy every night."

"Doesn't she worry about STDs and stuff?" I said.

"Old Betty who manages our apartment asked her that once, and you know what Tiffany said? 'My dad's a doctor.'" Chuck shook his head.

"What the hell good does that do her? How can someone smart enough to become a nurse be so naive?"

"Don't ask me. She's just an airhead, know what I mean?" He chuckled. "An airhead from the Windy City."

"Well, airhead or not, she sure has good pot." I stuck the roach into the hemostat-cum-roach clip that Tiffany had given me earlier and offered it to Chuck.

"No, thanks," he said, waving it away. "I used to smoke dope, but not anymore. I have an addictive personality, know what I mean? I like dope too much. Used to be always high. Then, when I'd play music, I couldn't remember what I was supposed to play. I kept getting lost in a tune and having to start it all over again. Drove the other guys in the band crazy. Besides, pot makes me paranoid. Makes me want to sit in a corner and dwell on all the negative shit in my life, know what I mean?"

7

"Yeah, I guess so," I said, pondering this revelation. A musician who doesn't smoke pot? How could this be? My New York-influenced skepticism gaining hold, I began to wonder if Chuck really *was* a musician. "So tell me about your music. Have you made any records?"

"I was in a band back in Chicago in the early seventies. We put out an album—*Watercourse Way*—but it was the classic rip-off. We never saw a penny in royalties." He stared thoughtfully at his wine glass and lit another cigarette.

"What was the name of your band?"

"Shadowfax."

"Cool. I think I've heard of you guys. What's your music like?"

"Electronic, instrumental. I play winds. We had bass, keys, guitar and drums." So far, so good. His details matched what Tiffany had said.

"Can I hear you play sometime?"

"Sure, but I'm not playing the same stuff now that I used to play with the

band. Since the bass player and I moved out here from Chicago, we've been working up some rock tunes."

"Where're you doing that?"

"We rent a hangar out at Santa Monica Airport."

"You play your own tunes?"

"Of course. Just finished writing one, as a matter of fact."

"Really? Sing it for me!"

"Nah, I have a terrible voice. But the bass player has a good voice. He does all the singing. Next time we rehearse, I'll take you over to hear us."

"Great!" I was interested to hear that there was to be a "next time." "What else are you into?"

"Poetry, especially John Berryman's. Now *there's* someone who really lived on the edge, but I guess it goes with the territory.

Want to hear some of his poems?" Without waiting for an answer, Chuck took a sip of wine, dragged on his cigarette, and began reciting:

Gentle friendly Henry Pussy-cat
smiled into his mirror, a murderer's
(at Stillwater), at himself alone
and said across a plink to that desolate fellow
said a little hail & buck-you-up
upon his triumph

"What do you think?"

"W-e-l-l," I said, batting my eyes at him and drawing him down with me so that we were now looking into each other's eyes. "First of all, I haven't a clue what that poem is about, but I am impressed at your memorization capabilities. Secondly, Tiffany didn't call you a 'pussycat.' She said you're a 'teddy bear with a weapon.' What did she mean by that?"

Chuck leaned over and in one movement began kissing me and slipping his hand under my shirt. "Wouldn't you like to know?" he said. As I listened to a screen door slamming in the wind, I thought, *What have I gotten myself into now?*

II

ANOTHER
COUNTRY

> The Chicago Four: G.E., Phil, Stu and Chuck—a scary bunch, seemingly drawn together as much by fear and loathing as love for each other.
>
> Alex de Grassi

The next morning, Chuck invited me to go garage saling with him. Over a breakfast of my huevos rancheros, he checked the morning L.A. Times and circled all the yard sale announcements within a few miles of Venice Beach. He also checked the used musical instruments section of the classifieds, which turned up one particular horn of interest: a 1941 Conn Ten-M Tenor Saxophone for two hundred bucks.

"Wow!" he said. "If this thing's in good condition, it's a real find!"

"Why?" I said.

"Because Conn stopped making it during the war when the government commissioned them to make war stuff instead. They needed bronze so badly that Conn melted down all the molds. Then, when they returned to making saxes after the war, they had to create new molds. Their postwar horns just aren't as good as their prewar ones."

"You know a lot about this stuff, huh?" I said. I hadn't heard him play yet, but I was learning to respect Chuck's business savvy.

"Well, I should," he said. "It's how I've earned my living for the past ten years. Let's go." I learned he'd been supporting himself by repairing horns for several local music stores as well as buying them used, fixing them up, and reselling them.

Next I knew, we were out the door, into the still-shuddering Santa Ana wind, and face-to-grill with "Ruby," as Chuck had dubbed his cherry red '65 Bel Air.

Ah, Ruby: the latest in a long line of vintage vehicles to be operated by Chuck. The bumper sticker read, "Another shitty day in paradise."

"I bought her literally from a little old lady from Pasadena," he said, more than a hint of pride in his voice. "She was in mint condition."

"Was?"

"She got hit by another car on the passenger side last week, so the door won't open. You'll have to get in on the driver's side and slide across. Or you can do what Tiffany does: Climb in and out through the open passenger window, legs first. Gives the guys a thrill, especially when she's not wearing underwear," he said, grinning.

Mulling over this image, I said, "Maybe we should take my car."

"No, really, Ruby's fine. All she needs is a spare tire."

"Don't tell me you've been driving around without a spare tire!" I gasped in disbelief.

"It's okay, I'll get one tomorrow." Chuck seemed astonishingly nonchalant about this, to me disturbing, fact. I'd been raised by an aerospace engineer father who was such a safety nut he'd made me take the train from L.A. to New York when I first went to college. He didn't trust airplanes because he claimed they were badly maintained. Before he allowed me to get my driver's license, I had not only to be able to change a tire but also to take a written test of safety and maintenance questions created by him. One of his cardinal rules was never to drive without a spare tire. But, well, rules were made to be, well, broken, and Chuck inspired a faith I couldn't explain.

I checked to make sure I had my Auto Club card with me, decided we could always get towed somewhere if we got a flat, then slid inside and across Ruby's front seat, thankful that it was a bench, not buckets.

The roads required careful negotiation as we headed to Culver City, site of the Conn Ten-M. The Santa Ana had left its typical flotsam: garbage cans rolling sideways on Pico Boulevard, palm fronds and eucalyptus branches littering driveways. Chuck provided a running commentary about his musical background as he navigated the Venice back streets, telling me about how he'd shifted his creative interest toward music after leaving high school, where he'd focused more on photography.

His initial independent foray began with a rental place on Stuenkel Road in Monee, Illinois, during the early '70s. With bands such as Chicago and Blood, Sweat and Tears gaining popularity, Chuck heard alternatives to the blues he'd grown up with. Music that featured hot horn sections had galvanized him, inspiring his own creative horn and wind concepts. He began trekking into the city, getting together with Jerry Smith, a bassist who had been gigging with The Flock.

Before long, Chuck had joined forces with some other musicians to form a band they called K.O. Bossy. They started out playing cover songs of the hits, particularly the Kinks. They would also do "Good Morning Little Schoolgirl" and other weird stuff. The guys in the band were big partiers and influenced Chuck to join in their laid back, hang-out lifestyle that was required for a happening rock band. They would play at a coffee house type of club called The Twelfth of Never in Richmond Park.

K.O. Bossy became a fixture at The Twelfth of Never and literally ran the place. They served the coffee, did everything—all the owners wanted was a cut of the "door." At one point the band decided to add a violin player, but they were still doing all cover stuff—no one wrote for the band, so they weren't doing anything really original—but they were like one big family. Although they recorded an album, it didn't propel the band to the stardom they had anticipated. According to Chuck's sister Suzin, the first pressings were off-center and produced a *wah wah wah* sound when they were played, although this has been disputed by a fellow K.O. Bossy band member. Needless to say, this didn't do much for record sales.

"Where did the band's name come from?" I wanted to know.

"K.O. Bossy was the name on the back of Curly Howard's bathrobe in a Three Stooges short," Chuck said. "I think it was called 'A-Milking We Will Go,' when the stooges put Curly in a milking contest. He enters the ring and has K.O. Bossy on his back."

One of those hanging out with Chuck in those days was Warren Flaschen, who, although two years ahead of him at Rich East High School, had not actually met Chuck there. One night Warren ordered pizza from Romano's, and the guy who delivered it to him turned out to be Chuck. They got to talking as Chuck handed the pizza to Warren and took his money. By the end of the evening Chuck was eating Warren's pizza with him.

Later, Chuck played with the McIan Forrest Stage Band, who went on to tour with the Bee Gees as their backup band, and when he returned from the Bee Gees tour he went back to delivering pizzas. This was when he wrote his first memorable—according to a longtime friend—song, "It's a Long Way from the Kitchen to Philharmonic Hall."

I wanted to know what it was like playing with the Bee Gees, my fascination with celebrities getting the better of me.

"Terrible. They were fucked up most of the time, and they only had me playing flute, when I really wanted to play sax."

After his stint with the Bee Gees, Chuck began showing up at the Situation Lounge in Steger. The Yazoo Shuffle Band played there, and that's how he met future 'Faxers Phil Maggini and G.E. Stinson, who were both in the band. Phil hailed from a neighboring town, Homewood, and had been playing in a group called Friends at the Valley View Young Adults Club in Frankfort. Friends got booked with a band called Mama's Bootleg Blues Band, which featured G.E. on guitar. It was Phil's first introduction to G.E. Friends had come on first and done a Paul Butterfield tune, then G.E. came on and said, "We're gonna open with a song the first band did but we're gonna play it the right way."

Eventually, Phil hooked up with G.E. in Yazoo Shuffle Band, and Chuck started coming around and jamming with them. Even though Chuck played a jazzy rather than bluesy sax—limiting the number of tunes he might do with Yazoo—they all liked each other, and a strong bond began to develop.

Like many bands, Yazoo's demise came about mainly through lack of funds to support the band members, but it didn't help that G.E. would often become visibly disgusted with the audience. One night in Bloomington someone in the crowd just stood up and screamed—really went wild—following one of G.E.'s guitar solos, although he didn't consider it one of his best. Contemptuous that the hapless fan didn't know the difference, G.E. walked to the front of the stage and spit on the audience, thereafter earning the nickname "Spit."

Once Phil, G.E. and Chuck began jamming together, the need for a keyboardist and drummer arose. The problem was solved when Warren began taking recording engineer classes in Chicago. He

15

befriended the teacher of the class, told him about the band's project and how they were looking for a drummer and a keyboard player who could play Mellotron. It so happened that Doug Maluchnik, a keyboardist who lived in New Jersey, had inquired about this course. Warren called him up, he came out and auditioned for the band, they decided it would work, and he joined up. At first he commuted between Illinois and New Jersey, where his family lived, but eventually they all moved to Illinois.

While Doug had never met drummer Stu Nevitt, he had heard of him. At that point Stu lived in Miami, played with a jazz group and took lessons from the same person who taught Bruce Springsteen's drummer, "Mighty" Max Weinberg. Doug contacted Stu who soon joined the rest of the band in Chicago. With the addition of Doug and Stu to the fledgling group, the as-yet-unnamed Shadowfax was complete.

The First Shadowfax, 1974: Phil, Doug Maluchnik,
Stu Nevitt, Chuck and G.E. [l-r]

Chuck finished his back story about the band as he deftly maneuvered Ruby around a downed power line that had partially blocked the road. He had proven himself to be a cautious driver, belying Ruby's impairments. However, I was beginning to wonder if

16

maybe we should have taken Blue Bomber after all. I glanced around Ruby's interior and noticed it was actually in pretty good shape, except for the headliner, which was hanging in shreds from the ceiling like seaweed.

"What happened to the headliner?" I asked.

"Oh, that. I took Phil for a ride after he had a fight with Tiffany. He took out his aggression on the headliner...with his fists. I guess he was a little pissed off."

"A little?" Before I could further question Chuck about the bass player, we arrived at our destination.

The Ten-M turned out to be the property of an old lady whose husband had died recently. She had discovered the sax in her attic, and Chuck noted it was still in its original case. The old lady said her husband had only played it a few times before going into the service, and when he returned from the war, he was a changed man, no longer interested in music.

Chuck considered this information and said, "Does it still play?"

"I don't know, but you can try it out if you'd like," she said.

Chuck wrested the gleaming horn from its case and began examining it with what looked to me like real tenderness, the way a mother might hold her newborn. He depressed each key, then reached for the mouthpiece.

"The keys seem to work and the mouthpiece still has a reed in it, but the cork's pretty shot," he said, twisting the mouthpiece onto the horn.

Then, lifting the sax to his mouth, he blew out some notes. They were only scales, but I could tell he knew how to play it. His tone was rich and confident. This guy really is a musician, I thought. But can he play anything besides scales?

Chuck put the sax back in its case, schmoozed the old lady for a few minutes, then offered her one-fifty.

17

"My son told me not to accept less than one seventy-five," she said.

"Okay," Chuck said, pulling out his wallet. "I'll take it." He counted out the money and handed it to her.

Grabbing the sax with one hand and my hand with the other, he thanked the old lady, and we exited into the wind.

When we had climbed back into Ruby, I said, "You really are a musician, aren't you."

"What did you think?" he said, glancing up and down the street. Without waiting for an answer, he said, "Let's go to my place," pulling Ruby onto Pico Boulevard and heading to Santa Monica. "I'm supposed to meet Robit there in a few minutes."

"Who's Robit?"

"A Jewish South African ex-pat musician friend. We've been working up some of his tunes."

"How did you meet him?"

"Phil and I were standing in line at a movie theater in Venice and Robit was right behind us. We hit it off right away."

"What kind of music does he play?"

"Robit is actually more of a poet/lyricist than musician. Kinda like Bob Dylan on a bad day. Phil calls him a master of the 'abused folk song.' But we need someone to play with, and he needs backup musicians. We're going to go over some tunes today to get ready for a showcase next week. There's a guy from Virgin Records interested in doing an album with him. Maybe we can get him interested in signing Shadowfax too. Or Eko-Eko."

"What's 'Eko-Eko'?" I said.

As we headed to Santa Monica, Chuck described Eko-Eko, the band he and Phil were forming. Chuck had written a couple of rock tunes which he had recorded with Phil and some other musicians. "Sensory Overload" was composed in his Santa Monica apartment one night while listening to the urban cacophony emanating from outside his window, a stark contrast to the quiet and peacefulness of the rural Illinois he had left:

> I live in a modern city,
> Twentieth Century all around me.
> Electric music is in my house.
> Voices of strangers come through my window.
> Traffic comes and always continues.
> My T.V. won't let me down.
>
> Down to the car and go to the store,
> My antique V-8 engine roars.
> Radio news tells me the score: sensory overload.

"Elevator Racing" evolved from a dream:

> We were elevator racing in the Empire State,
> To see how hot we could get the cable.
> Like living in a Frigidaire falling through space,
> In a twentieth-century fable.
>
> Because there's so few thrills up in the modern world,
> You feel so insecure.
> You've got to keep your head when the cable breaks,
> You've got to jump 'fore it hits the floor.

Chuck warbled the lyrics to me as we pulled into the carport of his apartment on Eighth Street in Santa Monica. The first thing to catch my eye upon entering Chuck's place was a baby grand piano that occupied the dining room along with a table upon which the artifacts of his horn repair business—instrument parts, saws, soldering irons and electrical wires—lay strewn. Globs of what appeared to be congealed glue covered the table. As soon as I stepped inside, I was immediately attacked by a small, truculent, parrot—a blue conure to be precise.

"Blue! Cut it out!" said Chuck. "Don't worry. He won't bite, but he might go for your earrings. He likes bright objects like that."

"Don't you keep this thing in a cage?" I said, feeling for my earrings and cringing as Blue took a few dives at my head.

"Yeah, but he prefers to have a run of the house and to sit on my shoulder while I work."

I glanced around at the disarray, wondering how much of it was Blue's responsibility and how much was Chuck's, not to mention his absent roommate Tiffany, who had not struck me as a neatnik. I could see that the curtains framing the kitchen and living room windows had been shredded at their edges. In some places, the curtain hooks had been pulled out from the rod. Blue had resumed his perch on the curtain rod in the upper corner of the kitchen window and chewed on one of the hooks, which he grasped in one clawed foot. This was obviously a favored spot for him—globs of what appeared to be his poop dripped down the wall and curtains.

Despite my trepidation at spending time in such an unsanitary environment, I was curious about Chuck's music.

"Play something for me," I said to him as he scurried around trying to make the apartment a little more presentable. "I want to hear what the lyricon sounds like. How about *Watercourse Way?*"

"Nah, I've never been happy with the way it turned out. But I do have a demo of something classical I did with an Oberheim synth player named Linda Nardini." With that, Chuck walked over to a reel-to-reel tape player in the living room and turned it on. What followed was the most indescribably ethereal and unique music I'd ever heard, despite the roughness of the recording. It had an amazing range, from notes high like a flute down to a low tone like a bass clarinet. Chills corresponding to the sound frequency ranged through my body outside my control, from the highs that tingled in my skull to the lows that rumbled in my belly. What kind of magic was this? Even with my untrained ears, I understood immediately that Chuck's was a talent destined for fame, if not fortune.

It was love at first sound.

Expert
Woodwind Repairs
10 years experience serving retail music stores...

Dealers prices

Overhauls

Flutes. *. $37.50
open or closed hole
Clarinets.. $37.50

Saxophones..
alto, soprano.. $70.00

tenor ...$80.00
restoring silver saxes
a specialty, prices higher

Bari, oboe, alto & bass cl.
prices on request

Free estimates, Pickup & delivery
ALL WORK GUARANTEED

All store stock 10% discount

Chuck Greenberg
Phone ...__394-3834

Chuck's repair flyer, 1980

21

III

ONE
WINTER
MORNING

.

> ...the violence and the unpredictability of the Santa
> Ana affect the entire quality of life in Los Angeles,
> accentuate its impermanence, its unreliability. The
> wind shows us how close to the edge we really are.
>
> Joan Didion, from "Los Angeles Notebook"

In a way, it seemed like we had dodged the first phase of "the game" before it had even begun. Chuck's spontaneity was a new experience for me. Somehow, it felt like I had known him for a very long time. What had begun as a not very promising blind date was looking like it might work into something more, despite—or maybe because of—the tension that is always in the air during a Santa Ana.

There is something downright disturbing about this Los Angeles weather condition known as the Santa Ana. It begins as an unnatural stillness that creates a foreboding—an expectation of doom that inspires some people to stay indoors, although they aren't sure why. Perhaps it is because of the accompanying rise in temperature, which often jumps into the upper nineties inland, excessively high for winter. It just doesn't seem right, even to the native Angelenos, to be celebrating Thanksgiving or Christmas when it's so hot.

And then, there's the wind. It can only be described as disquieting, like the mistral of France or the *foehn* of Switzerland. Or the smothering simoon of the Sahara. During a Santa Ana, the wind rushes off the high deserts, through the canyons, reaching hurricane force. It has such a parching effect that the fire threat becomes extreme. And if, God forbid, a fire does start, it's quickly fanned into a holocaust. It is not a benevolent wind; it's an alien wind. It's an alienating wind. It's a wind that, as Joan Didion says, "shows us how close to the edge we are."

Paradoxically, it's also exhilarating and full of possibility. Like the day I first met Chuck, when I had awakened in my beachfront apartment—not to the usual chanting surf, but to the cables clanging against the Venice Pier flagpole. Everything that had not been secured was now airborne, blown by the Santa Ana that had roared in from the east and buffeted the sailboats dotting the horizon. Last night's glassy sea had become a festering froth. The air felt electrically charged and static-filled, playing havoc with nature's equipoise. I'd heard that this was because of the unusually high ratio of positive to negative ions during the Santa Ana and the twelve hours preceding it.

That November day made me understand why so many people were willing to endure wildfires, earthquakes, smog and drive-by shootings to live in L. A. Surfers appreciated it for the offshore breeze that molds and holds up the waves, creating a fine, white spray of water that envelops like a lacy cocoon, or pipeline, as the cognoscenti call it. From my apartment balcony I could see wet-suited bodies lifted high, then plummeting down the glassy face of the wave. The mid-eighties temperature was ideal for lolling on the beach. The wind caressed without acting like a sandblaster. Sun worshipers had already formed a living patchwork in the sand.

An inexplicable excitement hovered like the gulls patrolling the tide line. Anything seemed possible on a day like this. I couldn't wait to slip on my roller skates and hit the Venice boardwalk. Soon I zipped along the bike path that meandered from Torrance to Santa Monica. Eight years earlier in 1972, the 18-mile bicycle path adjacent to Ocean Front Walk—the boardwalk that parallels the beach from Venice to Santa Monica—had been constructed. At that time, Venice was in a severe state of decay and in desperate need for redevelopment, thanks to a '60s policy of code enforcement that required all buildings to be upgraded to current building standards. Because many owners were unable to obtain the loans necessary to upgrade, 550 buildings—many along Ocean Front Walk and in the historic Windward business district—were razed. A lawsuit eventually stopped Venice's wholesale destruction, but it became a virtual ghost town except for the Beats and then Hippies who flocked to Venice for its cheap rent and tolerance toward pot parties, love-ins and drunken frenzies. It was during this period—in 1967—that I had attended a Doors concert at the Cheetah on the since-demolished Ocean Park Pier, memorable because of the terrible sound that was a fixture of pre-monitor technology.

Venice's rebirth in the '70s came about because the bike path allowed local residents to ride their bikes through the depressed parts of the city, bringing it new energy. Then, in 1976, the invention of the polyurethane skate wheel—which allowed easy gliding over concrete and asphalt—sparked the outdoor skating craze. Venice's wide Ocean Front Walk and bicycle path made it an ideal location for skating. Vendors began renting roller skates from outdoor lots along Ocean Front Walk, and tourists flocked to the area to experience the new sport. In 1980, I became one of those tourists.

25

From my starting point at the Venice Pier, I skated past an ever-changing cast of colorful characters, including One-Man Band who accompanied himself simultaneously with a variety of mobilized musical instruments, mutant body builders who frequented the fenced enclosure of weight machines known as Muscle Beach, Yiddish-speaking chess-players seated at concrete picnic tables in front of Synanon, and the Sheik—aka Harry Perry—a white-turbaned and robed, guitar-toting roller-skater who spun out Jimi-esque tunes with the help of his backpacked amp. Their vividness helped to distract me, for skating up and down the beach had become more than just an entertaining exercise. It offered an escape from the much more difficult work that I knew lay ahead of me: grief recovery.

* * *

I lost my parents and a baby sister by the age of thirty-one, and I had never come to terms with these events. The fact was I had come to feel less—not more—capable with each loss. Perhaps this was because I, like most Americans, had been taught how to acquire things, but not how to lose them.

I first became acquainted with The Last Enemy at the age of eight. My baby sister Tracy—born with a malformed heart before infant surgery was possible--passed away following a futile battle for survival. Other than a C-section, there had been nothing much eventful about her birth in 1956.

My mother decided to have Tracy at Good Samaritan Hospital in downtown L.A., then an hour's drive from our home in Whittier. A few days after Tracy's birth, my twin sister, Jill, and I went to the hospital with our dad, riding past tract homes dotted with orange trees. Soon the citrus orchards—once the ubiquitous trademark of L.A. suburbia—metamorphosed into oil fields, their rigs bobbing like giant mutant praying mantises.

The dipping sun created long, eerie shadows from the oil wells—stark profiles against the darkening sky. The hospital was like a huge hilltop castle glistening in artificial illumination, with a vast parking lot as its moat. All we kids could do was wonder and imagine what it looked like on the inside, for we—like all children in those days—were forbidden to visit.

So we waited in the car while Daddy went inside for what seemed like an eternity. Thirty minutes is interminable, of course, to seven-year-olds. We amused ourselves by singing songs and making up games to relieve our boredom. One of our favorites was Opposites. The rules were simple: we could say anything, however hideous or rude, so long as it was the opposite of what we really meant. It was our one opportunity to get away with verbal abuse that would otherwise be deemed punishable. I could say things like "I hate you and wish you would fall into a hole and die," and I wouldn't get in trouble. And Jill could respond, "Well, you're so fat you wouldn't even fit in a hole!" The first one to bring the other to tears won. It was an early lesson in passive aggression, at which we girls seemed to excel.

Daddy returned to the car with a look of relief on his face. Mommy and our new baby sister, Tracy Lynn, were healthy and fine. At least, she seemed so at first, but it proved to be a temporary illusion. Later we discovered that she was missing one of her heart chambers, causing her to have inexplicable convulsions beginning soon after her birth.

One of these episodes happened when I was changing her diaper. Tracy began crying uncontrollably, convincing my mother that I must have stuck her with a diaper pin—there were no disposables in those days. Then I started crying at being wrongfully accused, leading to mass hysteria in the Horner household. After several of these episodes, combined with Tracy's failure to grow in size, she was diagnosed with the heart defect.

27

When Tracy was nineteen months old, I awoke during the night to muffled sounds coming from her room down the hall. There were voices: one unidentified, low and masculine; one crying softly: Mommy's. Curiosity propelled me out of bed, stumbling in the dark, opening my bedroom door, blinking in the blinding lights from Tracy's room, spotting the large, tent-like structure covering her crib that had been placed in her room the week before. Even from my nine-year-old perspective, I knew something was wrong.

My eyes darted around the room trying to make sense of the incomprehensible: Tracy's crib covered with the half-opened oxygen tent revealing her absence and a police officer talking quietly and somberly to my mother, who was attempting to regain her composure through her tear-streaked, anguished face. For some reason, I went to school the next morning feeling not so much sadness as pride. Pride that this awful thing had happened but that I had managed to get through it and carry on as if death were merely a "badge of courage."

Horners in Seattle front yard, 1949: I'm on the left,
Jill's on the right, Daddy's in the middle

Once I had children of my own, I wondered how my parents held up so well when Tracy died. Then again, perhaps they didn't. Our mother tried to hide her grief from my sister and me, but months after Tracy died, while we were having horseback riding lessons, I caught a glimpse of her as we trotted like some live carousel around the paddock. She was deep in conversation with a friend and appeared to be weeping. I surmised it was about Tracy.

Like Tracy, my father might have been saved had medical technology been then what it is today. A victim of rheumatic fever as a child, his mitral valve was damaged, causing his heart to fail when he was fifty. Although the surgery to replace his faulty valve was a success, he was no longer able to perform the activities like hiking he had once enjoyed. In fact, he became bedridden.

Unable to accept a sedentary lifestyle, he sought a heart transplant at Stanford but was turned down, partly because of his age—fifty-two was deemed to old at the time—and partly because he and my mother were divorced by then and the post-op social workers didn't believe he had the support group behind him necessary to help him pull through the ordeal. Devastated by their refusal to accept him as a transplant candidate, he lost all interest in life. He died from pneumonia a month after being rejected by the program.

My mother was only a few weeks shy of retirement when she suffered an aortic aneurysm. Unlike my father and sister, there was nothing that could have spared her, so quick and catastrophic was her condition. She had no warning that anything was amiss, except for some back pain during the day. Then, at the dinner table, she said, "oh," and keeled over. The coroner said that even if she'd been on the operating table when her artery burst, they probably couldn't have saved her.

I guess I come from a family of weak hearts. Both my parents died many years sooner than they were supposed to, according to the national average life span. My father was fifty-two; my mother was sixty-two. How much did the stress of losing a child affect their health?

This is something I hope never to learn.

The grotesquery of Venice Beach, therefore, posed plenty of diversions from my grief. Besides giving structure to my daily routine, skating allowed me to observe—without becoming personally involved with—these beach creatures. Like watching a movie in fast-forward mode. To slow down was to risk connection—something I was not yet prepared to do, or so I thought. First, I needed to connect with myself.

Within a few months, I had lost my mother, my boyfriend and my job. And I had not yet finished mourning the death of my father ten years earlier. I was angry, although if you had asked me at the time, I would have denied it. Me? Survivor of a third of my life spent in New York—where if you can make it there, you'll make it anywhere? Former designer at the largest privately owned jewelry company in the country? Degree-holder from one of the most prestigious universities in the world? Surely, all that should have prepared me for anything. But, of course, no amount of book-learning or street smarts had readied me for loss. I had learned how to acquire stuff but not how to give it up.

Yes, I was angry. Actually, ANGRY. I was angry with Life, for dealing me this unforeseen and unwanted hand, when I hadn't chosen to play the game. I responded by self-medicating. My losses became excuses for self-indulgence. And what better place to debauch than Venice Beach? I lost little time immersing myself in a haze of drugs and alcohol—anything to deaden the pain. Since my arrival in Venice, I had devoted myself to getting—and staying—high. Much as I might like to point a finger for my waywardness at the raging Santa Ana and its positive ions, in truth they were my hands lighting the joints and holding the drinks.

On the other hand, negative ions—created by the tremendous friction that predominates at certain places like the seashore—produce positive effects on mood, energy, libido and sense of well-being. Researchers have supported the view that high concentrations of negative ions can increase both physiological and psychological arousal. Perhaps that explains why Chuck and I gravitated so easily toward each other, despite the malevolent wind.

Nah, we were just horny.

IV

EBONY
WIND

For something is never valued quite enough, until it has
ceased to be. To one side stands a man who dances in
the bamboo wind, screaming silver songs in reverse.

G.E. Stinson, from a poem

After much arm-twisting, I convinced Chuck to play
Watercourse Way—the first Shadowfax album—for me.
"Why don't you want me to hear it?" I said, when he kept
changing the subject.

"I've never been satisfied with it," he said. "Some of the tracks
just weren't up to par. It really needs to be remixed, but it's out
of my hands now."

"Why? What happened to it?"

"Passport Records has all the masters, and they're in New
Jersey. They don't have any interest in it any more. But if you
really want to hear it..."

"Yes!" I said. "I want to know if you're a real musician, or just a
wannabe."

Chuck was correct in his assessment of *Watercourse Way*. Many
of the tracks sounded frenetic, with all the musicians playing as
fast as they could but not really together. But there were two

songs I liked: the title track, and a sweet, Renaissance/folky sounding duet with Chuck on wood flutes and G.E. on guitar called "Petite Aubade."

"I like this," I said. "It has a catchy melody. Who wrote it?"

"G.E. and me."

"I like 'Watercourse Way,' too. Who wrote that?"

"G.E. and me. You'll have to hear us play it live. It's killer."

Clearly, Chuck and G.E. were the best composers on this album.

"What's that instrument you're playing on it?"

"Lyricon. Do you like it?"

"It's mesmerizing. I've never heard anything like it before."

"That's because there are only about three of us who know how to play it."

In fact, the lyricon provided a distinctive, signature sound for the band and projected a fluid lilt that soared with emotion when played by Chuck. Co-invented by electrical engineers Bill Bernardi and Roger Noble, a lyricon prototype fell into Chuck's hands in 1972. The venue for this serendipity was the Chicago National Association of Music Merchants annual show. NAMM shows are an essential staple for all serious musicians, and Chuck, like many serious music biz people, made it a point to check out everything new on display there. In fact, some of Chuck's most productive networking occurred at NAMM shows.

Bill Bernardi and Roger Noble were the first to ask themselves what might happen when they crossed a wind instrument with a synthesizer. Their idea was for a sort of "electric flute" that could be played in an orchestra and would allow the musician playing it to be heard all the way in the back of the hall. They formed Computone, Inc., to begin production of a prototype, never imagining that someone like Chuck would come along, plug it into a *wah-wah* pedal and an echoplex delay, and be heard around the world.

In 1971, Bernardi and Noble applied for a U.S. Patent on an "Electronic Wind Instrument," and three years later first mass-produced wind synthesizer, the lyricon, came into existence.

Coincidentally, Chuck had been looking for something that would add some "punch" to his musical contribution to Shadowfax. In the early '70s, he had been rehearsing with them at the Triple B, working up tunes written by G.E. that tended to be very riff-based, electric and aggressive. Chuck felt a bit ill-equipped to hold his own in this very intense, high-watt musical environment. He needed a new voice to express himself, and to compete with the level of angst in the little room—its windows covered with mattresses—that was the precursor to Big Burn Studios.

"When he came to rehearsal one day, he was just flipping out about this 'fucking spaceship' of an instrument he had seen at the NAMM show," said Phil. "He was elated and totally animated while he described what he thought was the answer to his prayers." Chuck worked with a prototype for a while and continued to develop the instrument with Bernardi as required by the music: a breath controller and then a bending reed to match G.E.'s blues-based sitar-inspired riffs. "It was always a trip to see this weird futuristic instrument, with a red bandana tied around its end to absorb Chuck's spit before it had a chance to run down the long silver shaft and short out an electric key pad. We had never seen or heard anything like it before."

The lyricon initially combined a Boehm-type controller—the instrument part that the musician manipulated—with a synthesizer—the part that actually generated sound. Both the controller, which resembled a twenty-inch-long recorder, and the synthesizer fit into a single, velvet-lined unit about the size of a sax case. As an already accomplished flute and sax player, Chuck recognized right away that it was an instrument of great potential for him, since the fingering system was identical to most flutes and saxophones. But, while the lyricon played similarly to a sax, there were two notable differences. First, the lyricon's reed did not vibrate—it only measured pitch. Chuck had to create vibrato and pitch bend by changing the position of his jaw against the reed in the lyricon's mouthpiece. Chuck had full dynamic control of the instrument's volume using only his breath.

Chuck demonstrating the lyricon, ca. 1974

Second, the keys were actually switches, and the bass clarinet mouthpiece only served to give the player the "feel" of a horn. Although there were some standard synthesizer controls that shaped the sound, most of the programming typified by a keyboard synthesizer was managed on the lyricon by playing: loud, soft, bright, mellow—whatever Chuck felt like. In this way, it was an instrument capable of truly reflecting its player's emotions.

The original Lyricon I was thus a wind controller which drove a computer that generated overtones. It had a shiny chrome finish with an elongated bottom piece and used a form of additive synthesis: Chuck dialed in the amount of overtones he wanted and then blended that with the wind-overtoned section. This model had a key switch for a fundamental of G, Bb, C, Eb or F and a range switch of low, medium or high. The three octaves on the instrument combined with two octave-up transpose keys on the control panel gave it a functional six-octave range. It also had glissando, portamento and "timbre attack," an effect akin to chorusing that allowed Chuck to play something like chords.

The notes were very expressive and there was quite a bit of player control over the actual sound. The down side was that—like with other early synths—there was no way to "save" a sound. So the first lyricon players had to know the way the dials should be set for a sound, and hope they remembered those settings. Another problem was its player's lack of control over any sound source other than the lyricon-operating computer. In other words, the player was limited to playing the lyricon only through its synthesizer. In addition, adding more of the top overtones could give it a very unpleasant, "buzzy" sound.

Furthermore, in order to mimic a guitar—necessary for the times Chuck and G.E. wanted to play the same notes together—the lyricon had to be able to effect two notes consecutively so that they blended together without sounding discrete, also known as "bending." Because of these limitations, Chuck worked with Bill Bernardi—who had split with Noble—to develop the Lyricon II.

With the Lyricon II and its built-in synth, Chuck achieved this goal. Although the Lyricon II looked different—it came in a plastic case and had a black, brushed aluminum appearance—from the Lyricon I, it kept the same sax style fingering and base clarinet mouthpiece with a sensor on the reed to detect pressure. Still, it remained difficult to master, which was why there were so few players. And there were no teachers; Bernardi and Noble were engineers, not musicians. They knew how to build the lyricon, but they couldn't play it themselves. Chuck mastered his essentially by

37

trial and error—adjusting the knobs and testing the resulting sound—a time-consuming process at best which necessitated years to develop.

The vicissitudes of travel made playing the lyricon even more difficult. Chuck discovered that changes in climate could render all his careful programming ineffective. For example, places of high humidity like Seattle and Portland would wreak havoc with the electronics. Fortunately, not everyone in the audience recognized the resulting sound as a mistake; some, in fact, thought the weird emanations were intentional. Once, during a show in Chicago, Chuck went into a solo when the instrument's electronics malfunctioned and he began blowing out the "skankiest off-the-wall tweets and bleeps, playing some horny moose, cows-in-heat, wildcat burning, fire-trucks-on-drugs impetuosity" according to Chuck's longtime friend Bill Johnston. "Some guy in the front row went into ecstasy, thinking Chuck was blowing a solo so outside it would take the roof off the place." He began screaming, "Ornette, Ornette!" thinking Chuck was the reincarnation of Ornette Coleman. "Afterwards, the man came up and couldn't stop telling Chuck what a powerhouse that solo was," said Bill.

Because of the difficulties with mastering the lyricon, it was a hard sell to musicians. This was compounded by its "electronic flute" image that tended to limit the imaginations of potential players, prompting Chuck to write a letter one time. The recipient's identity is unknown, but the message is clear:

To the editor—

Too often misinformation and opinion are accepted as fact by readers of an article. It is worse still when misguided opinions in articles are presented as fact by unnamed sources.

In the piece "Instruments of Ill Repute," the lyricon was singled out and described as "a gimmick, worthless," and as an "electronic flute." In reality, for a horn player, the lyricon is one of the most interesting and challenging instruments to be invented in recent years. It has vast musical potential, and if it is used as an "electric flute," it is only because of the limitations of the player.

The unnamed source is also quoted as saying he "saw the instrument in a big, expensive booth at a trade fair in Chicago." I also found it at a trade fair in Chicago—it was a very small display. The manufacturer is not some huge conglomerate but a small company in Massachusetts, run by a few dedicated individuals interested in expanding modern music.

What surprises me is that this person could see the instrument at all with such obviously limited musical vision.

Bernardi struggled to market the lyricon on more than a small scale. Although the Selmer band instrument company took over distribution in the early eighties, it was unable to market the lyricon successfully, especially once Yamaha and others began selling more competitively priced wind synthesizers. Bernardi eventually developed another company, Innovations Ltd., from Computone in Norwell, Massachusetts, but he no longer produces lyricons.

Despite these limitations, or perhaps because of them, the lyricon has become legendary. In 2003 I decided to sell on eBay one of three that Chuck had owned and played. On the first day I ran the auction, an intriguing response came from Chris Kraft, who lives in Boston and said that he was "a heavy metal guitarist in the mid-eighties playing the local club circuit when a friend had me check out a funny-looking album cover with the title *The Dreams of Children* by some band named Shadowfax. 'Who or what the heck is that?' I said. Just one listen and I was hooked. From start to finish, I listened to that entire album. I never do that with any new CD, even up to this day.

"I just recently got back into listening to Shadowfax after many years of exploring other types of music. Since working on my own album the past two years, I thought of that 'horn' sound that I loved so much in Shadowfax. My internet research to find out what the band was up to turned up this instrument called a lyricon. A quick trip to eBay revealed one of Chuck's instruments—it was a déjà vu type of feeling. At the same time I found the lyricon on eBay, I was reading Joy's e-book about Shadowfax. When I got to page ten, I received an e-mail message from her! I have to go place a bid on that damn horn now or I'll be haunted."

Thus Chuck became known as the most proficient of all lyriconists—the instrument that "looked like a vacuum cleaner," as guitarist Alex de Grassi described it, but "sounded like angels," according to Windham Hill Records founder Will Ackerman. Now that keyboard synth players have created "samples" of his signature sound, Chuck Greenberg and the lyricon are virtually synonymous.

V

NEITHER
HERE
NOR
THERE

Making the simple complex is easy. Making the complex simple, awesomely simple, now that is genius.

Charles Mingus

The thing that impressed me the most about Chuck in the early days of our relationship—even more than his sense of humor--was his commitment to music. Although I had been dabbling in the arts for years, I considered myself more of a dilettante than a true artist. Sure, I'd been a designer at a glamorous Manhattan jewelry company before meeting Chuck, but I'd never really sacrificed for my art. In fact, I'd sacrificed my art in order to please my parents. On the other hand, Chuck made it clear that his music came first—before me, his parents or anything else in his world.

Chuck's dedication meant that if I wanted to hang out with him, I'd have to alter my expectations for how certain things should be done. My first birthday shared with him was therefore spent driving reluctantly—at least, on my part—to a club in the San

Fernando Valley and meeting the owner, who was interested in booking Chuck's then band Eko-Eko. This was not exactly what I had in mind in terms of a celebration, but Chuck assured me that after he'd taken care of a "little business," he'd treat me to dinner somewhere. When the club owner learned that it was my special day, he looked at me with sympathy and said with a sweeping gesture at the mostly empty, quiet room, "He brought you *here* on your birthday? How about a drink on the house?" It was the only actual gift I got that day, although the time spent with Chuck proved to be only one of many entertaining ones to come.

Even so, Chuck's single-mindedness about his art inspired me to think the same way about mine. Since arriving in Venice, I had dedicated myself mainly to hedonistic activities. Although these pastimes worked to distract me from my grief for a while, before long I discovered that the essential problem with skating and getting stoned was they were but short-term solutions which yielded little permanent satisfaction. And so I returned to the activity which—unlike any other—had remained steadfast in its ability to help me transcend the ineluctable sorrows of my life: jewelry-making.

There is simply something thrilling about the entire process involved in the conception and fabrication of a piece of jewelry, from the initial gathering of elements to the holding and forming of separate objects into a finished, wearable piece. It is an endeavor that is psychically as well as kinesthetically rewarding. Long before I'd ever heard of "worry" beads, I'd learned that studying and fondling these small, colorful objects gave me far more satisfaction and pleasure than any other activity.

My attraction for jewelry began when I was in the second grade, thanks to a cereal marketing brainstorm that yielded Pop Beads. Made of hard, molded plastic, the pea-sized Pop Beads featured a shallow hole on one side and a nipple-like protrusion on the other that allowed you to snap them together, forming long chains. They came in a variety of colors, with my favorite being the pearlized version. I wore my Pop Beads everywhere, including school. No outfit was complete without being accessorized by a Pop Bead necklace, as my second through fourth grade class photos can attest.

Unfortunately, my girth expanded with my Pop Bead collection. So intent was I to own a necklace that color-coordinated with every dress I had, that I shoveled down cereal in order to find the small packets containing the individual Pop Beads. Soon I began popping out of my clothes, prompting my mother to stop buying the cereal. She substituted it instead with MetriCal cookies, those compressed wafers that tasted like sawdust, despite tantalizing flavors such as "chocolate fudge" and "French vanilla."

Sensing my dismay at the termination of my new artistic hobby, my mother bought me a little kit that contained enough materials to string three necklaces and told me she'd get me more supplies when I'd lost enough weight to fit back into my school dresses. I became hooked on bead stringing and vowed to do whatever it took to satisfy my new habit.

My first visit to a bead store required an hour-long drive into downtown L.A. The store was situated across from a dingy Greyhound station in a derelict-populated neighborhood, but once inside I found myself mesmerized by the rows of shelves containing every imaginable size, material and hue of bead. By now I had entered high school and had graduated from plastic to glass. I was especially fond of the faceted type and became elated when I found some in a burnt orange shade that matched perfectly the swatch of material I'd brought from a dress I'd sewn.

Despite their initial support for this artistic endeavor, my parents were less than thrilled when I decided to become a professional jewelry designer. My mother, the ever-pragmatic

43

English teacher, said, "You can be an art teacher, but it's not a very good idea to be a professional artist. It's too hard to make a living." My father was more succinct. "You'll starve," he said, knowing how much food meant to me.

"But I don't wanna be an art teacher," I wailed.

"Okay," he said. "Then be a doctor. As long as you don't waste your high grades and fine intellect on art, which is a great hobby but a lousy profession."

In truth, it was my father who wanted to be the doctor. Following his own mother's urging, John Wilbur Horner had become an engineer instead. My grandmother had noticed my father's precocity in the mechanical realm when—at the age of eleven—he took apart a Ford Model A and put it back together again, just to learn how a car worked. He'd had to do it by himself since there was no one in his household to show him how. His father had died during the flu epidemic of 1918 before my father was born.

His high grades at Atlantic City High School in New Jersey combined with dire financial need earned my father a scholarship to M.I.T., where he majored in mechanical engineering, graduated in 1941 and took his first job working for Chrysler in Detroit. He hated this job and complained that his bosses were "old farts" who weren't open to new ideas. He despised Detroit weather even more than his job and used to tell me that "as soon as the snow melted from the tarmac," he hopped the first plane out of town. He headed west where the weather was mild and the aerospace industry was booming. Armed now with an M.S. in physics from U.C. Berkeley and a new wife—my mother Eleanor—John accepted work at the newly formed Jet Propulsion Laboratories in Pasadena. In a letter written to my mother's father asking for his daughter's hand in 1944, he explained how his salary at JPL—a whopping three hundred and seventy-five dollars per month—was more than enough to support my mother.

The JPL job launched my father's career as a rocket scientist, but he still wasn't happy. After World War II ended, the government forced the aerospace businesses that had benefited from lucrative wartime contracts to employ military people, most of whom were not trained in engineering. Having to take orders from such ignorant supervisors really "griped his ass," as he liked to say. He realized that if he were the boss, he wouldn't have to listen to anyone, and therein was born his appreciation for doctors and careers that allowed for more autonomy than the one he had chosen. It was an awareness he determined to impart to me. "You've gotta work for yourself," he repeated so often to me, it became a mantra.

And so I headed for Barnard College in the fall of 1967 to study pre-med. My father had selected Barnard for me after discovering that it produced more female medical students than any other college in the nation. While it had a great pre-med program, the only art classes were in art history.

Sightseeing in NYC, '67

My would-be career as a medical doctor became imperiled right off the bat during my first semester at Barnard. Overwhelmed by the competitiveness of my chem classmates—most of whom had taken chemistry in high school, which I had not—I barely managed to eke out a C-, and then only because I earned an A in the lab, which balanced the Ds and Fs I got on the tests. For someone who had earned straight A's in high school, the discovery that I couldn't hold my own at Barnard was a humbling experience.

I promised to get tutoring the second semester, but this plan was thwarted when the Columbia University riots intervened during the spring of '68. How could I study chemistry when I'd look out my dorm window to see mounted police chasing antiwar demonstrators down Broadway? When the scent of revolution, not to mention mace, filled the air and far more exciting developments were taking place in the streets of New York than in my textbooks? When I found myself as a nineteen-year-old three thousand miles from home and the watchful eyes of my parents for the first time in my life?

I'd arrived at Barnard without much interest in politics, but the Columbia riots opened my eyes to the realities of the Vietnam War, as well as the Black Power movement. Not only was I forced to think about things that I'd been sheltered from during my safe, suburban, lily-white childhood, I was encouraged to experiment with my new friends. Although I'd like to blame my academic problems on the Vietnam War by rationalizing that it made us all crazy, in all fairness, it could just as easily have been the myriad other distractions that lured me from my studies, including drugs. Especially drugs. I smoked my first marijuana joint on Halloween of '67. It was love at first toke. From there I added LSD and would pride myself on how well I could maintain my composure while tripping. I enjoyed watching the looks of surprise on my friends' faces when I'd mention casually—sometimes after being with them for several hours—that, oh and by the way, I dropped a tab before I came to visit them.

46

I adopted the uniform of the sixties student as well: jeans and T-shirt. I had brought a trunk full of nice clothes, including a baby blue cocktail dress with spaghetti straps I had made because such apparel was on a list of recommended clothing, but I don't remember wearing it even once. My parents were horrified when I returned for Christmas in '67. Said my father, "We sent you to New York to get some culture, and you've come back a bigger slob than you were before." This comment stung, but not enough to make me change my clothes—or my ways.

Last, but not least in the pantheon of distractions during my freshman year, I had my first sexual encounter. The son of an old family friend from Connecticut was my first real boyfriend, although I apparently read more into the relationship than he did. We parted ways a few months after meeting.

The only thing that kept me from flunking out after my first year of college was Barnard's decision to allow students to drop any course they were failing Spring Semester and to take the rest Pass/Fail, which would not be counted in their GPAs. And so I dropped chemistry and just barely got a Pass in calculus.

Now that medicine was out of the question, I began considering other options for a major. I had always enjoyed writing, but had been discouraged from a career in journalism by my high school news staff advisor, Mr. Shoop, who had talked about how difficult it was for women in the field. Perhaps his comments were directed only at me, because my fellow, female, coeditor of the high school newspaper went on to a successful career as a New York City journalist. Perhaps Mr. Shoop really meant that I wasn't good enough to be a professional writer.

Whatever, my doubts about my writing abilities were reinforced in Freshman English at Barnard, where I found myself in the same class with others who also fancied themselves as writers, including Mary Gordon. Mary's efforts were consistently lavished with praise by our instructor, Miss Prescott, who wrote things like, "I think you're capable of better work than this" on my papers. My being a laborious writer and an even slower typist in those pre-word processor days didn't help, either. Writing papers was just too damn hard and time-consuming.

In order to make up the units I had lost when I dropped chemistry, I decided to take Psych 101 during the summer session following my freshman year at Barnard. It was a subject I had enjoyed in high school and it was being offered at Rio Hondo Junior College, the local community college for students in Whittier. This turned out to be a good choice. Not only was I fascinated by the course reading, I found my classmates to be far less competitive than those at Barnard. In fact, the course was so easy that I managed to score the highest grade on the final exam, even though I had forgotten to bring my notes with me for the open book test. It was a badly needed ego boost.

When I returned to New York in the fall, I changed my major in the hopes that my father would find psychology—taught as an experimental science at Barnard—a palatable alternative to pre-med. However, problems continued to plague me during my sophomore year at Barnard. My parents, who had not been getting along very well for several years, decided to divorce. Although my father had been confiding his plans for quite a while, the news rocked my equilibrium, driving me further into drugs and away from my studies. Still, I managed to finish my coursework for the year, albeit with less than stellar grades.

Experimental psychology proved to be almost as challenging as chemistry, with lengthy write-ups due for each lab project. It was like writing a term paper every two weeks, a time-consuming requirement that put a large crimp in my style. But I found the material fascinating, attracted as I was to learning about what makes people tick. I began considering graduate school and a career in research.

Nowadays Barnard offers a visual arts major, but I had to wait until my senior year before I could take a studio art class, and then only Pass/Fail. After all, it would be unseemly for an institution like Barnard—which prided itself on its challenging academics—to give equal weight to an A earned in painting and an A in chemistry. I loved the painting class, although I felt guilty indulging myself with a course my father considered meritless. Upon graduation, I made plans to attend Cal State Los Angeles in the psychology master's program.

Meanwhile, my creative interests became relegated to the back burner of my future plans, to resurface years later during the early '70s when I found myself living the hippie dream by collecting unemployment benefits in San Francisco. Inspired by the local street artists, I began collecting shells, feathers and other natural oddities—anything that could be turned into a bead or strung. I taught myself to macramé with nylon carpet thread that came in a rainbow of colors and formed a strong chain but was fine enough to slip through small bead holes. This thread had the additional advantage of being much cheaper than metal wire.

Although I was not very successful selling my macramé earrings and necklaces, I found it to be a relaxing pastime that I could return to often whenever life became too stressful. Like that period in 1980, the year my mother died and I broke up with my second boyfriend, with whom I'd been living for seven years. And because his parents owned David Webb, Inc., the Manhattan jewelry store where I'd worked as a designer for four years, I had lost my job as well. So here I was, back on Unemployment again, but this time in Venice Beach. With this charming, dedicated musician named Chuck.

VI

STREETNOISE

I remember:
Chuck as an amazing Christmas tree one Halloween;
we plugged in his lights and he was the
Smash of the Party.

Nancy Kulp

Although I was definitely not a virgin when it came to drugs, knowing Chuck widened my chemical horizons considerably. He may have given up pot smoking, but when I first met him, he was participating in a UCLA drug and driving experiment that paid him money for the "job" of taking pills and alcohol. It was helping him pay the bills for a while after he first moved to L.A. and—by featuring temporary, part-time hours—allowed him to spend more time getting his band together. He got me to enroll in the experiment as well and together we would drive over to some warehouse-cum-laboratory in Culver City where they would thrust us behind a driving simulator for a few hours and test our reflexes. We were given either the tranquilizer Ativan or a placebo, and on the last day they gave us screwdrivers to down in three minutes, at eight in the morning. Much to the consternation of the researchers, both Chuck and I tested as better drivers post-vodka.

Evidently, we were throwing off their results. They still paid us, however, and it had been so easy that for a time we considered becoming professional experimental guinea pigs.

"Only in the Land of Lah," Chuck said. "Lah" was a fitting phonetic nickname for L.A. he thought, where everyone and everything seemed possible.

This taught me that, in case there was any doubt, the drug gossip surrounding musicians was true. For whatever reason, the musicians I met through Chuck were chemical consumers, and to be around them was to live within an ambiance of altered consciousness. But I had no idea just how crucially this would figure into my future until one particular day.

I had known Chuck for about six months. We were not cohabiting yet, but we were spending most of our time together. Chuck was a popular guest everywhere he visited, and my place on the beach just south of Venice Boulevard was no different. One day, my housemates and I decided to throw a big party on Venice Beach. Featured prominently among the appetizers were some recently acquired magic mushrooms, a popular *hors d'œuvre* of the times. A few hours after consumption, quite a few spaced-out partiers wandered around. Chuck was one of those who had gotten especially high, at one point hallucinating heavily. As the sun set we watched footprints in the sand metamorphose into slithering snakes. Chuck began to interpret this as an omen of doom.

"Joy, I think I'm dying," he whined.

At first, I thought he might be exaggerating since I had discovered that he did possess a tendency toward hypochondria. But as he was becoming increasingly morose, I tried talking him out of it.

"You're not dying physically, Chuck, you're simply experiencing ego death," I said. No stranger to mind-altering substances, I recognized his death fixation as a classical psychedelic phenomenon and whipped out my copy of *The Psychedelic Experience.* I began reading excerpts to him in order to convince him that he was not really dying.

"Listen to this," I said. "One of the commonly reported physical sensations during ego-loss is 'Body disintegrating or blown to atoms, called fire-sinking-into-air.'" Following Leary's instructions, I spoke in a low tone of voice in Chuck's ear. "Does this sound like what you're feeling?"

"I'm m-e-l-t-i-n-g," Chuck said, doing his best falsetto imitation of the Wicked Witch of the West.

"Well, yes," I reasoned, trying not to laugh. "That's Physical Sensation Number Six: 'Feelings of body melting or flowing as if wax.' Don't worry—you'll be into the Clear Light soon." Then I proceeded to recite the Instructions for Physical Symptoms from the book:

> O friend, listen carefully.
> The bodily symptoms you are having are not drug-effects.
> They indicate that you are struggling against the awareness of
>   feelings which surpass your normal experience.
> You cannot control these universal energy-waves.
> Let the feelings melt all over you.
> Become part of them.
> Sink into them and through them.
> Allow yourself to pulsate with the vibrations surrounding you.
> Relax.
> Do not struggle.
> Your symptoms will disappear as soon as all trace of ego-centered
>   striving disappears.
> Accept them as the message of the body.
> Welcome them. Enjoy them.

Fortunately, this strategy worked, and Chuck's panic subsided enough to enable us to drag ourselves over to our favorite haunt, Zucky's, in Santa Monica for something to eat. It would be safe to say, however, that Chuck did not enjoy a "condition of balance, of perfect equilibrium, [or] of oneness" as predicted in the book.

Afterwards, convinced that I had "saved" his life, Chuck decided to "reward" me by proposing marriage. Having heard him once tell me, "I'm never getting married," I believed it prudent to suggest that he wait to see how he felt after a good night's sleep. As I drifted off that night, I remembered what a psychic had once told me: I would marry at 32. Realizing that this was my present age, I panicked. Oh, my God! Now what have I done?

Chuck and me in L.A., 1981,
courtesy of Benjamin Lesko

* * *

Chuck and I began spending most of our time together and decided it would be sensible to live together. There was only one problem, and it was a very sizable one: Tiffany. If I were to move

54

in with Chuck, it would mean extricating Tiffany, since she was still Chuck's roommate. The three of us sharing living space together was unthinkable—the apartment was simply too small.

Now, Tiffany had an ideal situation and she was not eager to change it. In Chuck she had found the perfect roommate: Someone who was discreet and not given to telling tales. Although we gave her six weeks to find a new place, it became apparent that we were going to need something tantamount to exorcism to rid us of her presence. At the end of the sixth week, when I moved in, she was still there. There were two hellish weeks when all of us were living in the same small place. Tiffany would alternate between her sweetness and light persona (in the hopes of convincing us to let her stay) and her darker alter ego. She finally wheedled and cajoled Phil into letting her move in with him, beginning one of the more infamous periods in the already notable career of Boyz Town.

* * *

It would be hard to find a greater den of iniquity than Boyz Town--the West Coast reincarnation of the Triple B Charm Farm in Crete, Illinois, named for Phil "Pretty Boy" Maggini, Warren "Honey Boy" Flaschen and another pal, Bobby "Sugar Boy" Murray. In the early seventies the three had moved into an old, drafty farmhouse south of Chicago that proved to be ideal because of its spaciousness and economy. It had a living room that measured at least eighteen by thirty feet and glistening wood floors, accented by knotty pine paneling. The Triple B had a bedroom area sixteen by twenty-eight feet and another room that later became known as "The Black Hole of Calcutta Lounge," complete with imitation Tiffany lamps and bar, brown vinyl couches and chintzy plastic stuff hanging from the ceiling. A moon and stars had been carved into the wall of a stairway that led to the upper floor bedrooms, so it became known as "The Stairway to Heaven." The three roommates' nicknames were immortalized forever when their friend Bacon, who was delivering tombstones for a living, had one done up for them with their three "Boy" nicknames—hence, the Triple B.

Triple B Charm Farm ca. '72: Sugar Boy, Pretty Boy and Honey Boy [l-r], by Chuck Greenberg

When they moved into the Triple B, the total monthly rent was $195, which included the house plus eighty acres. They could make all the noise they wanted without bothering a soul. The isolation allowed for many parties and provided the ideal place for bassist Phil to rehearse with the newly formed band he'd been playing with. Soon Phil, Chuck, guitarist G.E. Stinson and drummer Stu began rehearsing seriously in the basement room they dubbed "Big Burn Studio."

With Warren acting as manager, the band booked its first gig at Luigi's, a scummy little bar in South Chicago Heights, but the group still had no name. Then Phil got a call from the club owner the day of the gig. He needed a band name for his billboard, so suddenly they were pressed to come up with something. Phil started going through his bookcase, thumbing through books for a simple, direct name that would do the job. That's when he grabbed *The Lord of the Rings*, and "Shadowfax" popped out of the page. He hadn't read the book yet, but he discovered on this page that it was Gandalf the Wizard's enchanted horse, and it seemed to fit. The guys agreed; Phil called Luigi and told him he had a band name for his billboard. When they got to the gig, Luigi had misspelled it "SHADOW FACTS," but the club was already open and overflowing with people, and he wouldn't change it.

Pretty soon, they were gigging all over the Midwest. They put out *Watercourse Way,* things were going great. Then along came the disco craze, and their gigs dried up. It was 1978, and things were looking bleak. Whatever their sound might be, it was definitely not disco. They were no longer the musical flavor-of-the-month, and since they couldn't cover 'Night Fever,' they had to forget about getting any gigs. They just couldn't keep the momentum going.

Halloween at the Triple B, 1975, [l-r]: Sheik Warren, Xmas Tree Chuck, and Phil

"Also, there was this little problem of lack of sound equipment," said Warren. Their expensive P.A. had vanished, along with their sound manager, both later surfacing at the Park West, in Chicago. It seems that the sound manager needed a dowry in order to obtain his new gig as the in-house Sound Man, so, without asking,

57

he installed the Shadowfax P.A. there. It was hard to gig without a P.A., and putting together a new one cost more than they had.

The defection of keyboardist Doug Maluchnik proved to be the coup de grâce for the band. His wife had been pressuring him to leave the extreme insecurity of the music business for something more economically stable back home in New Jersey. With no work, no keyboard player and no sound system, Shadowfax fell apart.

Chuck went back to his old job repairing horns, but he was chafing at the lack of music opportunities in Chicago. The concept of a move to the land of gold records and Grammys started to gel in his mind. He convinced Phil to make an exploratory foray to L.A. in the fall of '78. They drove their rental car from San Francisco south to check out the coast and combine business with pleasure. Chuck wanted to stop every five minutes along Route One to take pictures. Eventually, it got dark and they ended up driving seventy through Big Sur, missing the whole thing, just to get into San Luis Obispo at a decent hour. But they felt in their guts that L.A. was the place to be.

Once back in Chicago, Chuck started making plans to move to L.A. permanently. He sent band manager Warren on a scouting expedition to shop the latest tapes that had come out of Big Burn, but he couldn't get anyone interested in the band at the time— Shadowfax was so outside and different from anything else that was being done. The band had evolved a non-melodic mode which consisted of "how fast can we play, how out can we get, how many time changes can we rip through." The response from the labels: "We might take a chance if they'd played with Miles Davis, but..."

Undaunted, Chuck decided that he would move west anyway. However, there was one major obstacle: money—specifically the lack of enough to finance this endeavor. Somehow, he managed to turn this monumental personal quest into a kind of universal life experience which all of his friends were obliged to experience along with him.

"I've always believed you should do what is right regardless of the risks," he said. "So even though I had no idea how I'd be supporting myself in California, when my cheapskate employer at the music store began bouncing my paychecks, I realized that this was one of the few ways to quit and still be eligible for Unemployment Insurance. And that's just what I did. I was able to use my unemployment benefits to bankroll my move to California."

Warren and Phil followed a few months later and moved into a house in Culver City. Although it appeared to be a typical tract house in a quiet neighborhood, the motley assortment of vehicles out front indicated that its inhabitants were anything but a normal suburban family. A VW bus perched on blocks in the overgrown lawn, and an old, multi-dented Harley sat in the driveway. And that was just the outside. Going inside Boyz Town was like entering Dante's Inferno. A small sign above the front door read "Beware of Dog." Someone had scratched an "s" next to the "g." I always hesitated before entering, unsure what danger lurked behind the closed curtains, or which disease might befall me if I touched anything.

Once inside, I was afraid to sit down—it was the sort of place where you might expect booby traps or, at the very least, whoopee cushions. And then there were the inhabitants of Boyz Town: Warren, Ronnie—another Chicago transplant—and Phil, aka "Little Boy-Boy," as he was fondly called on his bad days. Instead of a table, a huge perch dominated the dining room where two birds, Diablo and Hitchcock, hung out.

Each time he visited, Chuck greeted the birds and opened his mouth wide. To my horrified astonishment, Hitchcock, a good-sized cockatiel, crawled inside and began picking contentedly at the remains of Chuck's latest meal. This was at once repulsive and

59

fascinating, and I watched, transfixed, as did Hitchcock's sidekick Diablo, a large white cockatoo.

Numerous legends abounded about Hitchcock and Diablo, who was quite articulate. One time he had carried on a conversation with the hapless UPS man.

"Whaddaya want? Whaddaya want?" screeched Diablo.

"I just want to drop off a package," said the delivery man.

"Whaddaya want? Whaddaya want?" Diablo had a limited repertoire, and after a few more exchanges like this, the UPS man drove off, scratching his head in wonder.

Besides the birds, Boyz Town became notorious for its "theme days," which would occur at the spontaneous suggestion of its inhabitants. Drummer Stu, who lived on and off at Boyz Town, enjoyed "Hawaiian Day," when everyone would wear their aloha shirts. "Godfather Day"—inspired in part by Chuck's magenta fedora—allowed the guys to dress as their favorite gangsters and inevitably led to Godfather video marathons, accompanied by Chuck and Phil's verbatim recitation of the lines from the movies.

* * *

Yes, those walls of Boyz Town could tell quite a story, if only they could speak. Then again, perhaps it's just as well that they can't, now that the former inhabitants have all married and left or died. While discretion and taste have influenced the commission of some stories to memory only, there are a few things I can relate here. I was told that Diablo, in a fit of avian frenzy, eventually attacked and killed Hitchcock. Phil moved to the Hollywood Hills. Warren got a new job in San Luis Obispo. Ron lives in Oxnard. Stu bought a condo with his wife Sheri in San Clemente. And in one of those ironic twists of fate, the house on Marcasel is now an AA meeting place.

VII

MUNDUNUGU
(THE SORCERER)

[A reed is] a living thing, a weed, really, and it does contain spirit of a sort. And they say these areas [where reeds grow] make sound when the wind comes. It's really an ancient vibration.

Steve Lacy, *Saxophone Journal*

Chuck's sense of adventure led to a variety of interesting escapades, many of which transpired while traveling. I had only known him a few months when he decided to buy a VW van in Chicago, drive it to L.A. and sell it, profiting by the premium on vehicles in car-crazy California. Chuck had been making frequent trips to Chicago to visit his dying father and was looking for ways to offset the airline fees. When he spotted the VW van, he knew at once it would be an easy resell with a cheap vacation thrown in to boot.

The plan was for me to fly to Colorado, where we would meet and drive home to L.A. together. Our first stop was at a small ranch south of Denver where Dan—an old friend from Chicago—raised rabbits and insisted that we take a fresh carcass home, despite the length of our impending journey and Chuck's abstinence from meat. Chuck didn't want to offend Dan by refusing his generous gift, so we picked up a Styrofoam cooler and loaded the rabbit into it, packed with ice.

On I-25, climbing into the mountains and crossing into New Mexico, we discovered the van's heater didn't work. And we needed it. Although it was late March, the seven-thousand-foot elevation caused the temperature outside the van to plummet. I put on every garment I had brought with me but was still cold. Chuck sang songs and told jokes to distract me from my discomfort all the way to Taos, where we stayed that night.

Perhaps the most memorable part of the trip occurred as we headed west through Arizona from New Mexico the next day. We had decided to stop at the Grand Canyon, passing through Painted Desert at sunset, after taking the scenic route up Highway 264 through the Hopi Indian Reservation. We were not disappointed— the desert landscape, punctuated with cinnamon mesas, giant saguaros and vermilion-flowering ocotillo, was at its springtime finest. It was a time of year that Mary Austin's love of the desert could be readily appreciated, when "none other than this long brown land lays such a hold on the affections. The rainbow hills, the tender bluish mists, the luminous radiance of the spring, have the lotus charm."

A roadrunner attempted to keep pace with us as we zipped along the desert floor and up into the mesas. Reputed to be aggressive, ribald and devil-may-care, the roadrunner reminded me of Chuck, who was not big on domestic responsibilities either. He had already told me, "I'm never getting married, and I'm never having kids," a remark which led me to respond, "Fine. In that case, I'll keep dating others besides you." It was a moot point, however—it remained to be seen whose bluff would be called first. We were not dating anyone but each other.

Aside from the antics of the roadrunner, all was still and quiet in the desert. By mid-afternoon we had reached Second Mesa, a tiny Hopi trading post situated atop the geographical landmark of its name. Second Mesa seemed an unlikely spot for a town, given its remote starkness, but the austerity and vastness of the landscape emphasized the visual impact of every plant, rock and arroyo. As the late afternoon sun angled across the town, we decided to stop and stretch our legs.

We discovered that the Hopi art offered for sale in Second Mesa reflected its surroundings: pottery and baskets in the neutral gray, brown, black, cinnabar and sand of the indigenous flora and fauna. Long enamored of native art, I began browsing among the shops. I found items of great beauty, but the prices were high and I began to give up on the idea of purchasing a memento of our trip, now that I was unemployed and mindful of my expenditures.

One shopkeeper asked if we'd seen a young Hopi woman with a baby. I said no. The shopkeeper said this woman had a basket she was peddling but had been unsuccessful finding any shops interested in it; they were all stocked up on baskets at the time. The Hopi mother needed diapers for her baby and might be willing to sell her basket at a good price. We thanked the shopkeeper and went looking for the young mother through the nearly deserted shops and courtyards of the trading post.

After a few minutes of wandering, we began to notice the lengthening shadows and realized if we were to keep our original appointment with the setting sun on Painted Desert, we'd have to get going. Just as we were about to climb into the van and head off, a young girl who could not have been out of her teens came up to us, bundled baby in tow. With apparent difficulty mustering the courage to speak to a pair of white strangers, she asked if we were looking for baskets. When I said yes, she produced one from a ratty-looking brown paper bag.

I admired the basket, noticing right away the telltale Hopi style and craftsmanship. I asked her if she made it; she nodded affirmatively. I complimented her artistry, noting the symmetry of the design and coiled construction that featured perfectly spaced, alternating black and cinnamon stylized sheep on a greenish straw background. The basket was about three inches high by six inches wide and, as is customary, tightly woven enough to hold liquid.

I knew that basket making was a fine art among the Hopis. The fact that basket making was closely tied to nature and its elements appealed to me also. I found that knowing the creator behind the art contributed to its allure, and Chuck and I marveled at the versatility of reeds for making music as well as vessels. Thus motivated to engage this young Hopi artist in conversation, I asked her how long it had taken to create her basket. She said about a month, working on it in between caring for her baby. She shyly explained the process of gathering the reeds and grasses of different colors needed for this particular design, and how reeds are considered sacred by Native Americans because of their versatile functionality—so much so that they have found a place within Navajo cosmology as the origin of life, which began with a magic reed.

Holding my breath, I asked her how much she wanted for her basket.

"Thirty-four dollars," she said.

"I'll take it," I said, trying not very successfully to hide my enthusiasm. I had seen similar baskets in the Second Mesa shops for five times the price and recognized my good fortune. She seemed to recognize hers as well. We made our exchange, thanked each other profusely and took our leave. Chuck knew it was a bargain also; for once he did not urge me to haggle over the price.

Soon, we were passing through Painted Desert, now shimmering from a saffron sun that oozed like a broken egg along the horizon, casting elongated purple shadows from mesas and cacti across the boundless golden sands. We reached the first lookout over the South Rim of the Grand Canyon just as our Great Star bid adieu: a perfect finale to a magical day.

Later in the evening we were ensconced in a motel room overlooking the canyon itself. Chuck dragged the bed over to the window so he could ponder the depths of the abyss while concurrently making love. We enjoyed ourselves with an immensity that paralleled that of the canyon, although I couldn't help but think that the zenith of our trip—rabbit notwithstanding—had been our serendipitous encounter with the Hopi Basket Maker. And I marveled at the enchantment that seemed to accompany us whenever I was with Chuck.

Upon our arrival home, I cooked and enjoyed a delicious meal of *civet de lapin*, by myself, since the only meat Chuck ever touched was fowl. True to form, he sold the VW bus to Ronnie of Boyz Town at a profit, thus covering all his travel expenses.

VIII

SKYTRAIN

...no minor disaster ever felt disastrous when Chuck was along.

Mark Bernstein

The VW bus and his current ride, Ruby, were only two of many old cars operated by Chuck, who especially adored Chevys. In fact, I've never been certain that his lust for Blue Bomber, the '55 I inherited from my maternal grandmother, was not the real reason he married me. He prided himself on the collection of "beaters," as he called them, that he had run through over the years. Ruby—the candy apple red '65 Bel Air coupe that was in near-mint condition until Chuck got his hands on her—was but the latest in a long line of beaters to be operated by Chuck.

Many Chuck stories involved wild rides in whatever beater he was driving at the time. Longtime pal Bill Johnston was living in Park Forest the summer of 1970 and working on the railroad when Chuck called him up and asked if he wanted to go up to Chuck's Wisconsin property for the Fourth of July with two friends, Pat Caporetto and Mark Bernstein.

"Chuck came by to get me at my parents' place," said Bill. "He drove up in a 1950 Chevy pickup truck with IVAN WALKER AND SONS, MONEE, ILLINOIS stenciled on the doors. I asked Chuck

67

about the truck and found out he'd purchased it that very day. 'How much did you pay?' I asked. Chuck laughed at me and said, '$75. Isn't it great?' It was not an auspicious beginning to our trip."

In fact, the truck was not great at all. "It was rusted out along the panels, and it smoked something terrible," said Bill, "but it was 1970, we were all crazy, and we'd all read On the Road. We got in the truck. Actually, Pat and Chuck got in the cab; Mark and I piled in on the sleeping bags in the back, and we began our journey all the way to the northernmost border of Wisconsin at six p.m. in the evening. The truck was blasting out tons of blue exhaust, but the motor sounded okay, so we settled back, Mark and I cracked a bottle of wine; we settled in for adventure."

It was at the Stoughton exit, about 50 miles from the border that the adventure started. "The oil pressure gauge suddenly dropped to zero, and we careened down the exit and made it into the first filling station off the Interstate. We discovered we were down a gallon of oil, which suddenly brought the huge blue cloud behind us into perspective. We discovered the Ivan Walker got twenty miles-per-gallon and fifty miles to the quart. We bought four gallons of bulk oil and headed off again in the pollution mobile.

"Around midnight we drove past Stevens Point and picked up two hitchhikers, who got in the back, and I got up front with Chuck, who was afraid to let anybody else drive the truck, because he didn't know if the steering would go, or some other disaster would overtake us, and he wanted to be driving when it happened.

"Under some questioning I found that his first story about how much he paid for the truck was not quite true. It turned out he paid $50 for the truck and used the other $25 to bribe the safety inspector at the truck inspection station to give him the tabs to drive it. Needless to say, this was information I could have done without.

"By 3:30 or so, I was punching him in the arm to keep him awake while he sang a spontaneous composition he called 'Down Home Chinaman on the Farm.' He was a tired Greyhound driver, and we were only to Tomahawk, where we stopped to let off the hitchhikers, add more oil again, have some sandwiches, wine, and rollyerown. By about five a.m., we were in Minocqua, where, as the only vehicle on the road, we attracted the unwanted scrutiny of the Minocqua police, who followed us all the way through town, just to make sure we were leaving. At least it woke up Chuck for the last 80 miles. We made his property about 6:30 a.m.—a twelve-and-a-half hour drive.

"The property was beautiful, and we played around on it for the balance of the day, then took ourselves over to Ursula Schram's, who owned a farm nearby. She let us sleep there for the night in a room she was remodeling. We laid out our sleeping bags and passed out on the floor.

"Sunday we got a good breakfast at some cafe in Ashland, played at Lake Superior, where there were fifteen people on a beach below the cliffs, and where one guy said he'd never seen so many people on the sand at one time. We slept at Ursula's again that night.

"Monday, we started back and stopped at a Paul Bunyan restaurant in Merrill. It was an all-you-can-eat place, and we got our money's worth—plus there were three incredibly beautiful Wisconsin babes working as waitresses there and we had a great time flirting with them and found they were all quite ready to run away with four crazed hippies in a 1950 truck. It was information we stored for later.

"I don't remember much about the drive back until we hit the Interstate just north of Schaumburg, where an ex-Marine Illinois State Trooper pulled us over because he didn't see any license plates. When he saw the applied-for paper in the windshield it

69

pissed him off, and he gave us a tirade about backing up traffic for miles and kicked us off the Interstate for no good reason, other than we offended his sensibilities.

Chuck in Wisconsin, early '70s,
courtesy of Jeff Paris

* * *

"On the highway we now had to use there was a Schaumburg Policeman waiting for us who pulled us over again, checked Chuck's license, the safety inspection sticker, then asked if Chuck had flares and reflectors. Well, actually Chuck did have flares and reflectors, and the cop was really pissed about that, so pissed I almost laughed, which would have been a big mistake, but he had to let us go, so we went and Chuck spent the rest of the trip going back to that supreme moment when the cop asked for the reflectors and Chuck said, 'Sure,' he had reflectors and dug them out of the panel boxes of the truck and fried the cop's ass.

"'He thought he had me when he asked for flares and reflectors, Bill, but I had him on that one.' For someone like Chuck who easily fixated, that was a big moment. It was the first trip we made to Wisconsin, but it wouldn't be the last—Chuck made at least two more trips up there in the Ivan Walker—and all the trips were bizarre and incredible."

Childhood friend Mark Bernstein enjoyed several memorable trips with Chuck as well. "I had known Chuck forever, it seems," Mark said, "which is almost true as we were in the same kindergarten class, attended the same high school, and saw each other thereafter whenever I was in Chicago, or whenever his band got to Ohio, where I live. We spent a fair amount of time together during Chuck's pizza-delivering days in Chicago Heights, when he was playing with K.O. Bossy and was chagrined when the company that put out the band's only album would not sign off on the title, *A Ten-Minute Break While We Bring in Fresh Cows*. I remember a trip the two of us and a friend of his named Kenny made one Fourth of July weekend to some land Chuck for a time owned near Lake Superior.

"It was incredibly hot, and as we scrambled around his land we got sticky and scratched up and decided that nothing on the planet would be more satisfying in that wholly vacant spot than to strip down and dive into the lake. Which we did, and from the exact instant the leading edge of our fingertips made contact with the surface of the lake, we knew we had made an irretrievable mistake. Nothing, nothing anywhere, is as cold as the water of Lake Superior, even on the Fourth of July.

"I remember in particular a car trip he, my then wife, and I took from Ohio to New Orleans years ago one December, and of Chuck taking his instrument to play in a small unmarked club several blocks north of the tourist traps. I recall that he much wanted to play there with musicians he thought well of, but also how anxious

71

he was to respect the fact that it was their stage, and he was not going to crash it, or seem to. And I think his sense of respect communicated itself—that he was there for music, not to show off—and he ended up playing with them and playing marvelously.

"We cleared out of New Orleans on New Year's Eve, just a few hours ahead of the expected flood of Texans heading to town for the Sugar (Cotton?) Bowl. As we headed for Chicago, it was seventy degrees and balmy. We reached southern Illinois at two a.m. in time for a horrendous snowstorm. At the best of times, southern Illinois is a rather desolate place, and now it was completely closed down. The only safe thing to do was to continue driving through the night at twenty miles an hour up the unplowed Interstate until we got to the city. My first thought on this excursion is that no minor disaster ever felt disastrous when Chuck was along."

Chuck with one of his "beaters,"
Chicago Heights, '77

* * *

Jeff Paris also knew Chuck in the early seventies. "At the time," Jeff said, "Chuck never owned a car that had any business being on the road. One summer day Chuck called me and asked if I could help him run an errand. He wanted me to follow him to an auto junkyard. His latest car had developed suspension problems and he wanted to be rid of it.

"I had a firm policy of never getting into any of Chuck's cars, standing still or moving. They were instruments of imminent disaster. So when he called I tried to beg off, figuring the safest place to be was always two highways away from the one Chuck was driving on. But Chuck was a hard man to say 'no' to, and I ended up at his house inspecting the ailing deathmobile.

"The deathmobile was of unknown origin. The word collage comes to mind, as it seemed to be constructed of disparate car parts. It looked Japanese and there was a Datsun logo on one side panel, but the hood ornament belonged to an Alfa-Romeo, if I recall correctly. A sea of rust, all the car panels had detached from their welds.

"When Chuck engaged the engine, I was surprised not only that it started, but that the engine sounded good. Chuck floored the accelerator a few times and, tires squealing, headed off to the junkyard with me following behind. When he swung onto a curving expressway ramp, I was amazed to see the body of the car shifting left while the frame and wheels went right. Everything settled back into place once he had it pointing straight. He drove fast for several miles before veering off of the expressway. This time everything shifted in the opposite direction.

"A half-a-mile short of the junkyard and going about thirty miles an hour, the deathmobile suddenly dropped its nose while dark smoke started pouring from the wheel wells. Chuck managed to get it stopped and when I came up to see what had happened, he was laughing and pointing at the shock absorbers and mounts, now protruding about four inches through the top of the rusted front panels. The smoke came from the tires rubbing against the car body.

"Undaunted, he jumped back in and drove slowly to the junkyard, thick clouds of dark smoke trailing behind. When we arrived, Chuck tried to turn into the entrance only to find that his car no longer turned. The junkyard had to use its tow truck to bring it in the last hundred feet. When Chuck asked the yard manager how much he could get for the deathmobile, the man, shaking his head in disbelief, replied 'Well, after we deduct the towing fee, I figure you owe us about twenty bucks.'"

IX

THE
FIREWALKER

Suddenly there was this indescribable, ethereal
sound...the music of angels.

William Ackerman

Despite his business, automotive and musical skills, some
areas of life challenged Chuck. For example, it became
obvious that Chuck could not be bothered with the trivial
and mundane details of maintaining a household. As a result, I took
on most of the duties: paying bills, cleaning, cooking—anything that
might distract from his music. I quickly learned that if I didn't
perform these chores, they wouldn't get done. This would always
be my foremost problem with Chuck, for he never did interest
himself in tidiness.

However, his many wonderful qualities more than compensated
for his slovenliness, reminding me that, after all, there are far
worse traits than sloppy housekeeping. For one, he was the most
affectionate man I'd ever known. I cannot recall a single day
passing that he failed to say "I love you."

Furthermore, Chuck did manage to figure out a way to cover
expenses while striving to make it as a musician. His horn repair
business, cultivated while living in Chicago, continued to flourish.

75

Once he worked on Clarence Clemons' sax. It was a rush job since Clemons was in town with Bruce Springsteen and needed it for a gig that night. Clarence was so grateful to Chuck that he sent him a pair of tickets to the show. I was thrilled—Springsteen was one of my favorites. But Chuck gave the tickets away; he was rehearsing with the band that night and wouldn't let them down, not even to hear The Boss. I was disappointed but at the same time impressed by his dedication to his career.

The *Cash McCall* Band in Pasadena, 1982: G.E., Phil, Morris Dollison, Stu and Chuck [l-r], by Pax Lemmon

There soon evolved a microcosmic musical community that could provide work for a lot of people. The timing was perfect—it became a little engine, allowing everyone to play and record with each other. Phil and Chuck became creatures of habit, starting a rehearsal schedule with a day-in-day-out routine, knowing the process was essential to their growth and viability as musicians. Robit did, indeed, manage to attract the backing of a label and cut the album *Resident Alien* with Chuck, Phil, drummer Stu Nevitt and guitarist G.E backing him up. By then Stu and G.E. had moved out from Chicago and were rehearsing with Chuck and Phil in a variety

76

of bands, including one fronted by another old friend from the Windy City, Morris Dollison, aka Cash McCall. The Cash McCall band featured all the blues songs, like "Sweet Home Chicago," the guys had grown up listening to and playing.

It was through this musical network that Chuck's—and Shadowfax's—Big Break arrived. Robit had met another guitarist, Alex de Grassi, in London, where he was playing music in the streets, subways and folk clubs during the summer of '73. Robit had kept in touch with Alex and had been urging him to collaborate somehow with Chuck.

Meanwhile, Alex had established himself as the premier solo instrumental guitarist on the seminal New Age label, Windham Hill. As Windham Hill cofounder Will Ackerman's cousin, Alex was in an influential position, something that did not go unnoticed by Chuck. He admired Alex's artistry and was eager to meet him. The feeling was mutual; Alex sent Chuck the tape of a guitar part to a new piece he was working on and invited Chuck to contribute a lyricon part. Chuck was only too happy to oblige. Then one day in the latter part of '81, Chuck, Robit and I drove up to San Francisco from L.A. in Ruby. I dropped them off at Alex's house in Noe Valley and went out to visit some friends while Chuck and Alex rehearsed some tunes for Alex's upcoming album *Clockwork*. When I returned later, I heard a gorgeous melody emanating from Alex's as I parked the car in front. It was the song, "Clockwork."

Alex was impressed as well. They ended up recording two pieces. "Everybody went apeshit," Alex said.

Indeed, they did. It seemed that all who heard Chuck's lyricon were enchanted. Alex's album Clockwork scored a big hit on radio and at retail, as well as with the powers at Windham Hill. As a result of its success, Chuck was emboldened to propose an album to Will Ackerman, who initially believed that Chuck wanted to do a solo project. Chuck's task became convincing Will that what Will really wanted was a Shadowfax album, something he managed to accomplish without Will's ever hearing the band play.

Chuck sensed that Will would not approve of the "outside," heavily electrified, screaming-for-attention tunes that had been recorded by Shadowfax on *Watercourse Way*. It just didn't jibe with the primarily acoustic, mellow, laid back sounds for which Windham Hill was gaining recognition. And Chuck knew better than to invite Will to a showcase and see this "electric fusion monster quartet"—the antithesis of Windham Hill music—live. It would have been an invitation to disaster, sending the self-avowed hater of electronic music running for cover. Will's interest in recording Chuck was based upon Chuck's essentially acoustic approach to Alex's record *Clockwork*. To accept this offer on the basis of Will's perception, completely ignoring the nature of his label's musical direction, and to present him with an electric manifesto, would have been unfair to him and deal suicide. No, meeting and hearing Shadowfax was definitely not the way to get a deal with Will.

However, the band had a card up its sleeve—one it could play without any negative sense of compromise or loss of musical integrity. There had always been an acoustic side of the band that they very much enjoyed but that was never allowed to come to fruition. Now they simply took advantage of the opportunity to explore it further, creating a discipline that was at once challenging and creative. Chuck figured out how to convince Will that Shadowfax would be the perfect ensemble addition to the label's roster of solo artists.

Fortunately, Will Ackerman was so smitten by Chuck's lyricon from the moment he heard it that he was willing to go ahead with Chuck's plan to record. "Suddenly there was this indescribable, ethereal sound," Will said. He and Alex were sitting in a park in Silicon Valley, listening to "Clockwork," and this "unbelievable sound, the music of angels." Alex told him that "the angel responsible for this sound was one Chuck Greenberg, and that the instrument was called the lyricon." When Chuck joined Alex in concert at the Great American Music Hall, Will was there, and "there was that sound of angels again." After the show he spoke with Chuck, who promptly told him about Shadowfax, and it was decided, more or less on the spot, to record a Shadowfax album.

At first, I was incredulous that Chuck would want to go to all the extra trouble to get the band back together: At this point I had never heard them play live.

"Why bother with them when you have the chance to do your own thing?"

"Because," he said, "I will always have the opportunity to do my own thing, but I may not always be able to work with this band. And we never finished what we started out to say."

After hearing the results of their first Windham Hill recording, I understood what he meant. There was something magical that happened whenever Shadowfax played together. When I listened to their music, I couldn't help but be transported to a higher plane of existence—a place where time stood still and all cares and worries were at least momentarily suspended.

The magic was not limited to the recording, either. Once the band finished in the studio, Chuck put his manager hat on and began ferreting out possible venues to present the new music. In early '82 he booked their first gig at a funky little club on the fringes of Marina del Rey with the unlikely name of Hop Sing's. I finally got to hear them play although not without some last minute excitement. The gig had to be postponed a few weeks when Stu became too ill to perform due to complications from his diabetes, but it was worth the wait. Shadowfax displayed a virtuosity on stage that surpassed even that of the recording, with a crafted set that began with softer numbers like "Angel's Flight" and "A

Thousand Teardrops" and built to the rousing closer "Brown Rice." The concert's highlight for me, however, was "Watercourse Way," from the first, long lost Shadowfax album of the same title.

"Watercourse Way" featured Chuck's trademark lyricon and began as a graceful, playful romp and built to a break when Chuck switched deftly to alto flute. The flute then carried the lilting melody to an emphatic conclusion. The tune showcased Chuck's skill at changing instruments in the middle of a song without distracting from the performance. Jamii Szmadzinski on violin added a rich and rounded texture that was missing in the song's first studio version. Until Chuck composed "A Pause in the Rain" a few years later, I most looked forward to the part of the set when the band played "Watercourse Way."

X

RITUAL

Jew, non-Jew, doesn't matter. The body doesn't matter. It is the soul itself that is Jewish.
Nathan Englander, "The Gilgul of Park Avenue"

As might be expected wherever Chuck was concerned, our wedding morphed into a comedy of errors. It was the day after Thanksgiving '81. True to Murphy's Law, everything that might have gone wrong did. First of all, our wedding rings did not arrive, despite assurances from the salesman that we had ordered them in plenty of time. This actually was not such a great tragedy since, being a jewelry designer, I had wanted to design them myself anyway. We had only selected a matching pair from the store because it was faster than getting them custom-made.

Secondly, the flower arrangement was not ready, although the florist did manage to get my fresh orchid hair ornament to me on time. No big deal; my sister agreed to pick up an arrangement on her way over to our Santa Monica apartment, where we had planned the event.

Thirdly, and potentially most disastrous, was the tardiness of our non-denominational pastor from the local church that specialized in interfaith unions. To kill time while waiting for him, we started on the champagne that was supposed to be for the

81

celebratory reception afterwards. We also began snacking upon a five-pound Hershey bar, a wedding gift from my ex-boyfriend. Our wedding party was purposely small, consisting of Chuck's mom, Janice, his best friend and bass player, Phil, my sister, Jill, and her husband, Don.

Several people knocked unexpectedly on our door as we waited for the errant cleric who had agreed to marry us. First, our friend, Warren, making the rounds in the limo he'd been chauffeuring, showed up. He had been driving Beach Boy Brian Wilson around nearby Brentwood and was on a break, so he decided to drop by. When Chuck opened the door and Warren saw us all dressed up, his chin nearly hit the floor. We had deliberately kept most of our friends in the dark about our wedding since we wanted to keep it small and didn't wish to hurt the feelings of those who weren't invited. Warren stayed long enough to share some champagne with us before heading away in the limo.

Next, Jungle John—one of Chuck's friends who'd just arrived from Guatemala—showed up unannounced. At J.J.'s suggestion, we cracked open more champagne, and in no time we were all quite tipsy, except for Mom, who could be seen looking worriedly towards the door in all the photos commemorating this fittingly chaotic event. Chuck was her oldest child and the last to tie the knot, and she was not about to go home to Chicago without witnessing its resolution.

Finally, after numerous phone calls and several hours waiting for Rev. No Show, it dawned on us that we would have to go to "Plan B" if we were to get married. After all, it was Friday, and we doubted we'd be able to find anyone to perform the service over the weekend. Besides, Janice needed to return to her job in Chicago on Sunday. But what Plan B? As some of us discussed the logistics of getting to Las Vegas, Don—the only one with any problem-solving skill remaining at this point—began calling the wedding chapels that proliferated along Santa Monica's Lincoln Blvd. Amazingly, on a day when many businesses were closed, he found one open. And yes, Rev. Lynch—her real name—would be only too happy to help out. Although Rev. No Show had our marriage license, Rev. Lynch assured us this was not a problem. She would be thrilled to provide us with a Confidential Marriage Certificate that was just as legal as the regular license, she claimed. I was skeptical, but what the heck, I thought, whatever works at this point. Rev. Lynch invited us to come right over.

Soon all seven of us crammed into my '55 Chevy, "Blue Bomber," which I had long suspected might be the real reason Chuck—always a fan of vintage vehicles—had proposed to me. Fortunately, we had only to travel a few blocks. After parking out front, we stumbled through a plastic plant-filled atrium whose tackiness triggered fits of laughter from the group, not to mention derisive comments from Chuck. Rev. Lynch quickly sized up our situation and admonished us for not behaving more respectfully regarding this hallowed event.

"You know, this is one of the most serious times of your lives. You really need to settle down," she said. But it was impossible to keep straight faces with Chuck cracking jokes constantly, saying things to Rev. Lynch like, "I hope you don't live up to your name." Always irreverent, he was truly in rare form that afternoon.

Eventually, we pulled ourselves together and Rev. Lynch asked if we preferred the "traditional" or "Native American" ceremony. Never being ones for the "'til death do us part" stuff, we decided on the latter. I don't remember much about the ceremony, except that I was crying by the end of it. The combination of champagne and emotion ultimately had gotten the best of me.

Afterwards, we drove to our favorite local restaurant, Le Petit Moulin, once again in Blue Bomber.

The following morning, Rev. No Show called in a fit of anguish over his lapse of memory. Janice took the call. "I'm so sorry," he said. "I simply found myself with what I thought was a day off from work and totally forgot. Did they manage to get married?"

"Yes," hissed Janice. "No thanks to you!"

* * *

A few days later, I applied to legally change my last name to Chuck's and needed a copy of the marriage license to do so. I discovered that, indeed, it was a Confidential Marriage Certificate, supposedly created to accommodate Hollywood stars during the '40s who had set up housekeeping together and didn't want anyone to know they were not already wed. All that was required to obtain such a license was signing a statement verifying the cohabitation of the couple; there was no need for blood tests. Only the two marriage partners could legally acquire this information. And only in the Land of Lah, as Chuck would say.

* * *

We had come from completely different backgrounds, but somehow, our relationship worked. Chuck was from a working class neighborhood on the South Side of Chicago; I grew up the child of educated, professional parents in a bedroom community of Los Angeles. Perhaps it was a shared culture of the sixties that brought us together—when Motown music, sex and politics combined to create a special identity for us baby boomers. Perhaps it was our common affinities for art and philosophy. Perhaps we recognized and appreciated in each other qualities we hadn't found in anyone else. Perhaps it was a combination of all these things, but one thing is for certain: it had little to do with religion.

Because I've always felt like a resident alien among Christians— especially the active proselytizers—marrying Chuck, who was

Jewish, did not require any particular "leap of faith" for me. In fact, I've always been more comfortable with Jews as a group than any other culture—not so much for their religious position as for their cultural orientation. Indeed, Chuck was an embodiment of all those traits I find so attractive in my Jewish friends: artistic, intelligent, compassionate, and funny. Ironically, when we met, Chuck was losing interest in Judaism just as I was gaining it. Along with the musical transformation that was taking place in his external world during the late sixties, Chuck was experiencing an internal transformation. Against the wishes of his parents, he had dropped out of college and begun focusing entirely on music while growing his curly red hair into a long, unruly mass. Causing further consternation within his family, Chuck began smoking pot and—although he had been raised in a Conservative household and had been bar mitzvahed—he stopped going to temple and celebrating Jewish holidays.

Chuck reciting at his bar mitzvah, 1963

Meanwhile, two thousand miles away in California, I was discovering Judaism while distancing myself from the birth religion of my parents: Christianity. I'm not sure why, but I never "got" Jesus. Perhaps it was my *laissez-faire* upbringing by a father who, forced to attend his local Methodist church in Ventnor, New Jersey, every Sunday as a kid, revolted as an adult and announced

85

that he would never return to church himself. He did, however, offer to take me if I wished to attend. Well, what kid would choose Sunday School over Sunday Sleep-in? And if regular churchgoing hadn't made him a True Believer, what could I hope to gain from it?

There were few Jews in my sheltered suburban locality when I was growing up. An important exception was my father's best friend Gary Gould, a fellow aerospace engineer who had fled Germany during World War II, lived in Brooklyn where he learned English (with a Brooklyn accent) and met and married another Jewish émigré who had hidden in a French convent during the war. Daisy Gould was a fabulous cook and the only person I've ever known who could create such culinary exotica as escargot with her own home-cultivated snails. She also made killer lasagna.

By having the Goulds as family friends, my father managed to renounce the anti-Semitic beliefs of his mother, who regaled us with stories about renting her house near Atlantic City during the summers to "rich Philadelphia Jews" who would invariably trash it. Because my grandfather had died before my father was born—leaving Gram strapped financially—these summer rentals provided much-needed income. And because she made it her home during the rest of the year, Gram took the carelessness of her renters very personally. Nonetheless, my father was not influenced by her anti-Semitic diatribes, and consequently neither was I.

How do children know when their elders are so off base with their biases that they should be ignored? Perhaps it is part of the ubiquitous rite of passage for teens who reject everything their parents say. And perhaps this is why Chuck was rejecting his Jewish past while I began embracing it. Whatever the reason, my father and I never took Gram's denunciations seriously. Her stereotyped descriptions and our own reality were totally at odds. After all, the Goulds were far more cultivated than the slovenly renters depicted by my grandmother. Furthermore, the Gould home was immaculate.

As much as I loved the Goulds, it was Anne Frank who really piqued my curiosity about Jewish culture. I fell in love with reading following my preteen discovery of *Diary of a Young Girl*. I fell in love with Jews, too. In my callowness, there was something tragically romantic about them that appealed to my own adolescent, unexpressed yearnings, something so *je ne sais quoi*. Inspired, I began keeping a diary myself. Never mind that my diary, unlike Anne's, was filled with sophomoric sexual references and drawings illustrating concerns that were rather different from Anne's loftier philosophical reveries. Anne's journal fired in me a desire for knowledge about Jews more realistic than what my Gram offered. And I knew this quest would not be satisfied within my WASP-filled suburban L.A. hometown.

Subsequently, it was my philo-Semitic father who encouraged me to attend Barnard College in New York City, despite the reactions of some who said things like, "why would you want to go to a place where there are so many Jews?" Little did they know, nor did I tell them, that this was precisely why I wanted to go there. Like Nathan Englander's "Gilgul of Park Avenue," whose protagonist's improbable epiphany in the back seat of a taxi convinces him that he is Jewish, I felt an immediate bond with my new friends. Indeed, I welcomed their esoteric contributions to my heretofore sheltered life upon arriving at Barnard in 1967, a move which proved especially fortuitous in that it was through my induction into the famed "Jewish Geography" network that I ultimately met Chuck.

After leaving New York in 1971, I moved to San Francisco where my friend Rob Mayer, who had attended Columbia at the same time as I, was living while attending Berkeley. Rob's brother Alan had rented a house in Marin with some fellow law students, one of whom had done his undergraduate schooling at Syracuse University and introduced me to another Syracuse grad living in S.F., Stanley Silberstein. Stanley and I became a couple and eventually moved back to New York, where his family owned and ran David Webb Jewelers. I worked there as a designer until 1980—the same year my mother died. When we broke up, I decided to return to L.A. It just so happened that Stanley's friend Joni Gildin had an apartment in Venice Beach—the very same place I met Chuck. Like I said: Jewish Geography.

I believe that Chuck's change in religious faith had to do partially with coming of age in the sixties. People now speak of a "loss of innocence" following the events of September 11, 2001. But Chuck and I—like many others like us—lost our innocence in the late '60s with the realization that a government elected to protect us was, in fact, lying to us, tear-gassing us, chasing us down the street with its mounted police, and even shooting at us with its National Guard. As SDS leader Mark Rudd said, "This revelation was more than we could handle." Fellow Weatherman Brian Flanagan put it a bit less euphemistically: "The Vietnam War made us crazy."

And so it was that Chuck—always interested in political science and even majoring in it for the brief time he attended college— lost faith in all institutions: religious, social *and* political. Our backgrounds may have been very different but about these concepts we were in complete agreement. We understood that our revered institutions had created an insane and unjust world and it was our responsibility to come up with something that worked better. I believe that the mutual experience of this chaotic time period, more than any other factor, is what bonded us.

Of course, I had to convince Chuck that the family institution was not as dispensable as religion and politics. When I had first met him, he had made a point of letting me know he was "never getting married and never having children. Little musician-killers" he called them. On the other hand, I—having lost both parents by the time I met Chuck—had decided I needed a family. And, armed with the belief that children of unwed parents are unfairly—and unnecessarily—stigmatized, I wanted to be married before having children. Needless to say, Chuck eventually changed his mind, albeit not without the proverbial kicking and screaming.

It did help to have the support of his family. In Chuck's mother, Janice, I could not have found a more ideal mother-in-law. My not being Jewish was never a problem for her. In fact, she told me that I was more Jewish "in spirit" than many "real" Jews she knew. The fact that I reinstated Passover and Hanukkah into Chuck's lapsed-Jew life was not lost on her. I suspect that she was relieved that Chuck—her first-born but last-wed—finally had gotten hitched. Whatever her reasoning, Janice welcomed me into her family. Her three other, younger children had already wed goyim—how could she complain about another one? Besides, I was "Jewish by injection," as Chuck liked to say.

I suppose that in some ways I am like John Berryman: an "Imaginary Jew," forced by circumstance to take positions on issues like Zionism and civil rights that stereotypically concern Jews. Fortunately, these days when I am asked if I am Jewish, it is not usually with the same apparent contempt and disdain as during Berryman's 1940s wartime America. Of course, anti-Semitism still persists, but I would like to think that in some small way I am helping to dispel the myths and prejudices about Jews which continue to prevail, particularly in the aftermath of the World Trade Center attack which has stirred up anti-Israel sentiment.

When I had lived in Manhattan in 1976 and the possibility of marriage to Stanley raised itself, I had toyed with the idea of converting to Judaism, but the commitment part always hung me up: I've never felt so sure about something that I could totally embrace it in the manner that "conversion" has always implied to me. For one thing, I'm a confirmed agnostic. For another, hearing some Jews snicker about converted shiksas "trying to out-Jew the Jews" did not enamor me of the conversion concept—an issue that never arose with Chuck.

My usual defense for taking Chuck's surname when we married, as opposed to following the feminist fashion of retaining one's maiden name, is that—in an eerie foreshadowing of his death—a paralegal had advised me once that having the same name as my husband would make it easier to collect his Social Security survivor benefits. However, in hindsight, I think the real reason I changed it was to become Jewish without "officially" converting. The simplest way to achieve this was to acquire a Jewish name.

Ultimately, however, by marrying Chuck I realized a long-standing fantasy: I got to experience vicariously being a talented, successful musician without having to endure directly the unpleasant, intimidating baggage—like going on the road—that went with this career. Seven months after our wedding I wrote in my journal that Chuck was "a 'dream come true'…the most compassionate, understanding, intelligent, attentive, talented, interesting, humorous, easy-going, happy, communicative, sexually satisfying person I know (or have ever known). I LOVE CHUCK!"

Chuck and me in L.A., 1981,
courtesy of Benjamin Lesko

XI

ALMOST
A
DREAM

as Shadowfax
relates the angel's flight,
poignant, delicate
with delight

shadows fall
away and light becomes
the way of wings:

stirring in rings
the waves of wind
and leaves to find
peace of mind
     Paula Kullberg, "Shadowfax: Shadowfax"

Chuck composed most of Shadowfax on the baby grand that still filled up the living room of our Santa Monica apartment. He would write the melodies, tape them, and send them to G.E. in Chicago, who would add the chordal parts. Sometimes they would even compose over the phone together. There was suddenly an intense mutual interaction that had only existed minimally before. Chuck had metamorphosed into a responsible guy who was doing all the right things to get the job done. It also didn't hurt being in the right place at the right time.

Despite their previous experience as hard-rockin' electronic wizards, G.E. and Chuck made a conscious decision to create an acoustic album for Windham Hill, knowing, however unspoken, that this was what the label wanted. This was no problem for G.E. since he had already composed a wealth of tunes on his acoustic 12-string guitar. Indeed, he welcomed the freedom to traverse new directions musically and to investigate the work that was being done at the time on the ECM label with the likes of Ralph Towner and Oregon.

Recording Shadowfax was an incredible feat. By promising to self-produce the record, Chuck had made an attractive, inexpensive package for Windham Hill. He had put together a budget of $12,500, which we raised by soliciting funds from friends and acquaintances. Using part of the inheritance from my mother, I became an investor as well. In return, we investors were given a "two-for-one" deal. In essence, each investor would be paid back from artist royalties earned off the record until all five of us had received double their initial contribution of $2500. It proved to be a sound investment: within a year we investors had both recouped and capitalized upon our initial investments.

We acquired a new roommate during this period. G.E.'s physical presence was now necessary, so he came out from Chicago to work on the album, staying with us until he could find his own place. It was fun having him with us—he was intelligent, articulate, and funny.

One night the smoke detector in our apartment went off, possibly from cockroaches or other vermin running around inside it. This had happened before, but it was particularly unnerving to have it happen while sound asleep. Chuck lurched out of bed, ready for combat with the ear-shattering foe. G.E. arose also, to see what the commotion was about. He opened his door to the hallway just in time to see a naked Chuck swinging wildly at the offending device.

"It's Australopithecus!" said G.E., who believed for a moment that he was having a prehistoric dream.

Chuck then managed to get drummer Stu out from Chicago also, tearing him away from his C&W gig and ensconcing him as the latest inhabitant of the nefarious Boyz Town. Although Stu had demurred at first, when told that erstwhile Weather Report drummer Peter Erskine was considering the gig, Stu changed his mind.

Soon G.E., Phil and Stu were rehearsing with Chuck, preparing the new tunes for recording. Since funds were tight, Chuck really had to search to find a studio that would fit his budget. They ended up at Studio America in Pasadena—extremely primitive as far as amenities were concerned, but sporting the necessary equipment to do the job to Chuck's specifications.

It was hard to believe that Chuck had never produced an album before. It came so naturally, even if it exacted a high emotional price. Musicians don't take easily to direction, and it required all of Chuck's patience and diplomacy to achieve the recording he desired. High sound quality was important to him—he wanted to please himself and all the audiophiles he knew were out there, and Windham Hill was building a reputation for crystal clear recordings as well. But even the best sound quality wouldn't matter if the music didn't match up. Fortunately, it did. *Shadowfax* featured exquisitely gorgeous compositions that proved to be a seamless addition to the Windham Hill catalog.

Response to *Shadowfax* was overwhelming. One person wrote that she had never written a fan letter before and tended to disapprove of any type of "idol worship. I have been searching for music that speaks to me, that is deep and meaningful, and that is timeless. Now I have your music to inspire me and console me. Thank you, Shadowfax."

Others sent their praise directly to Chuck, saying, "Never before have I experienced some of the highest life-principles through music, but your performance seemed the essence of beauty and truth and moved me beyond words."

A German fan wrote that he had "never found so much comfort and peace as in this record. The music's beauty is totally hypnotic; you are unable to resist the complex unity of rhythm and melody. It is an experience as if a magician has put a spell on me. Every time the needle hits the record I am drifting away, unable to do anything but listen."

As Chuck had expected and predicted, there were many who appreciated the superior sound quality as well as the music. In a letter to the band, one fan rhapsodized that he had purchased "audiophile" recordings for twice the price that had not sounded this good. "How can I express in words the joy that I felt when my stylus caressed the grooves of this record for the first time! There was no detectable surface noise. The music was so clear that it seemed each instrument occupied a distinct position on the frequency spectrum."

Those Shadowfax tunes were so radically different from any music that was being performed or recorded at the time that it was not surprising they evoked such emotional responses. Chuck had been careful to soften and restrain the harder edges of Shadowfax so that they would produce a sound more tailor-made for the Windham Hill catalog. This meant that all the tunes on *Shadowfax* were melodious and gentle, with subdued rhythms—virtually the antithesis of what the band had formerly been doing live back in Chicago.

The favored hit selection from *Shadowfax* turned out to be "A Thousand Teardrops." A lovely, lilting tune featuring a haunting Lyricon melody, "A Thousand Teardrops" went on to be included on several Windham Hill samplers. It was, and still is, one of the most popular of all Chuck's and Shadowfax's tunes.

Critical praise for *Shadowfax* was as ecstatic as its popular acclaim, despite the universal inability to categorize the music. Leonard Feather, the venerable late jazz critic for the Los Angeles Times, wrote, "Classifying this album is a tougher task than appreciating it. It is not free, folk or funk, not classical and minimally jazz, and not primarily improvised, though some cuts have a strong, loose rhythmic pulse."

Some of the listener confusion lay in the discrepancy between the laid-back, acoustic style of the record and the band's forceful, electronic stage presence. While Chuck was mindful of the need to give Windham Hill a record that would fit in aurally with the rest of the catalog, he, and the band, felt that performing live was another matter altogether.

Although there had been a concerted effort to tone down the more boisterous rock and blues predilections of the band for its new record, they felt they had carte blanche to allow the "rock monster" that lurked inside their collective psyche out, and in concert this band really rocked! Even Will Ackerman, when he finally heard them live, had to admit to liking it.

Nonetheless, those who would become familiar with the music through the recordings would end up invariably lumping it in with the rest of the Windham Hill artists into that category dubbed "New Age," a term forever loathed by Chuck because he believed it to be essentially a misnomer. Many listeners somehow considered New Age to be a reflection on some collective spiritual nature of all the musicians, a belief that Chuck was quick to debunk whenever he could.

Since Shadowfax was never a primarily acoustic band, Chuck thought it ridiculous to categorize them with the likes of Scott Cossu, etc. Chuck was especially incensed when the backlash to New Age Music began seeping into music reviews with comments like "hot tub music" and "yuppie Muzak."

As far as Chuck was concerned, the categorization problem lay not with the concept of New Age Music *per se*, but with the attempts to use it to define a cultural lifestyle, religion, or event. He objected vehemently to the fact that perfect strangers were making assumptions about his personal beliefs and attitudes based upon what kind of music he played.

New Age notwithstanding, Shadowfax found themselves with a hit record on their hands and the need to promote it. This meant putting together a touring band and a tour. Since no one else was so inclined, booking and road managing fell to Chuck. As G.E. put it, "I can't even balance my own checkbook."

* * *

For the first tour, which featured such "hot spots" in California as Chico and Cotati, Chuck rented an Itasca Winnebago. We used my American Express card since no one else had credit. Although I'd been employed for many years, American Express was the first company willing to take a chance with me, and only because my boss at the time personally vouched for me. I was therefore more than a little nervous about putting my meticulously cultivated good name in jeopardy, but I needn't have been. Chuck made sure every penny was repaid.

Besides the Chicago Four, Shadowfax's ranks had swelled to seven with the addition of keyboardist Jared Stewart, percussionist Adam Rudolph, and violinist Jamii Szmadzinski. To keep expenses down, Chuck had it figured out that some, but not all, of the guys could sleep in a hotel room, while the rest could share the Winnebago, using the hotel to shower. By the time eight guys (there was also a roadie) had finished with the one hotel room, it required virtual fumigating and remodeling.

Despite the hardship of the first tour, it was deemed a raging success, particularly since each member got to go home with a hundred bucks in his pocket. Chuck's emergent and formidable business acumen, which now included ad hoc booking agent, had made it possible to end up in the black, even though on-the-rise instrumental touring bands were not doing so at this time in the early '80s. It was something in which he would always take great pride: that he had never booked a money-losing tour.

An afternoon with Windham Hill at the Greek Theatre, Berkeley, 1983,
[l-r] George Winston, Michael Hedges, Liz Story, Andy Narell, Russ Walder,
Ira Stein, Darrol Anger, Barbara Higbie, Alex de Grassi,
Jamii Szmadzinski, Will Ackerman, Chuck, G.E., Stu and Jared Stewart

Besides the financial success of their eponymous album, the band's performances garnered critical acclaim. Concert reviewers and fans everywhere were praising the band's musicianship, once they got over the shock of hearing the tunes in their highly electrified stage versions. These early sets were comprised of cuts from both *Shadowfax* and the earlier *Watercourse Way*, along with tunes which had been previously written but never recorded. One of these, "New Electric India," was a G.E. composition that was deemed far too rock-oriented to be included on *Shadowfax* but always captivated audiences when played live. It proved to be a stunning showcase for G.E.'s wailing guitars and Jamii Szmadzinski's virtuosic violin, the latter performing an awesome, explosive mid-tune solo.

XII

MAKING
SHADOWS
DANCE

To Charles Greenberg––
You breathe the Breath of the Tao into Shadowfax!
Thank you, a Poet.

Anonymous, from a cocktail napkin

The success of *Shadowfax* enabled the band to go into production on a second album. For material, they didn't have to look too far. Intuitive businessman that he was, Chuck began thinking about all those old *Watercourse Way* masters over at Passport Records.

Although *Watercourse Way* had been out for eight years, the band had never received a dime in royalties. Chuck knew that there were many copies in print, however, and that the demand for them would increase with the release of the new *Shadowfax*. He also believed that if *Shadowfax* turned out to be a hit, there might be a renewed interest in the band's first album, *Watercourse Way*. However, he wasn't willing for Passport to be the beneficiary of any newfound success, particularly since he felt that Passport had burned the band for nonpayment of royalties. So, Chuck and the band's attorney Steven Lowy devised a scheme to buy back all the old master tapes. Chuck knew he'd have to move quickly—before the release of *Shadowfax*. Once Passport suspected it might be able to gain more mileage out of *Watercourse Way*, the price for the masters would go up.

It worked—Chuck made them an offer and Passport was only too happy to rid themselves of what they perceived to be a "dead horse." On the very day that the Billboard review hit the stands raving about *Shadowfax*, Chuck was collecting the master tapes from the Passport warehouse and blithely walking out the door with them.

Gaining the rights to *Watercourse Way* turned out to be more significant than even Chuck imagined at the time. In addition to re-releasing it *en toto*, Windham Hill selected one of its cuts, a lilting Chuck/G.E. duet called "Petite Aubade," to be on the first of their *Winter Solstice* series, which went on to achieve Gold Record status. It also made it possible to "borrow" those tunes which the band felt were basically worthy but which had not succeeded as well on *Watercourse Way* as they had expected. For this reason, the title song from *Watercourse Way*, along with G.E.'s "Song for My Brother" were selected to be rerecorded for the second Windham Hill Shadowfax album, *Shadowdance*.

As with *Shadowfax*, Chuck and G.E. shared song writing duties on *Shadowdance*, with the exception of a piece by Don Cherry which was a medley of two tunes, "Brown Rice/Karmapa Chenno." G.E., Phil, and Chuck were big fans of Cherry's music and had been performing "Brown Rice" live, traditionally as the closing number of their set. It was the only non-Shadowfax composition they ever recorded or performed, and likewise one of the few with lyrics. Nonetheless, it was a testament to the band's arranging skills. A consistent and perennial show-stopper, "Brown Rice" featured raplike (before it was in style) nursery rhyme lyrics growled out by G.E. and backed by his searing guitar, with Chuck screaming on tenor sax, building to a crescendo then switching to a wailing lyricon—all pushed forcefully by Phil and Stu's rhythm section.

Shadowdance became another showcase for Chuck's burgeoning production genius. Although it cost slightly more than *Shadowfax* to create, he brought it in on time and under budget. In addition to the seven touring band members, he enlisted Emil Richards in the studio again, with Michael Spiro and Mickey Lehockey to beef up the percussion. The title tune from *Shadowdance* went on to become a featured number live, often receiving the greatest recognition and applause whenever they performed it and deservedly so. "Shadowdance" combined all the best qualities of Shadowfax: a catchy melody, rhythmic beat and interesting assortment of instruments.

Virtuoso percussionist Emil Richards had filled up the whole room at Group IV Sound with his esoteric collection of instruments from around the world, and the result was astounding. "Shadowdance" became a consistently sought tune by filmmakers, TV and radio shows for background music. After more than a decade, it is still being used by the Monterey Bay Aquarium for what I call its "dancing plankton" exhibit.

The band was also now able to afford a better recording studio when they set out to do *Shadowdance*, finding in Group IV the perfect place financially, personally, and technologically. A few years earlier, Chuck had performed on a movie soundtrack at Group IV and managed to cut a deal for himself through the owners to use the place at night—traditionally "dead" time--at a bargain rate. Without Angel Ballestier and the rest at Group IV, it would have been impossible to cut such high quality records for the price. So began an illustrious multi-record liaison between band and studio.

101

* * *

Shadowdance was an immediate hit and more touring ensued. In 1984, the band had arrived at a small East Coast college town, and Chuck and Phil decided to warm up by downing Schnapps. Thus fortified, they grabbed a local newspaper to see if anything had been written up about the band. What they discovered was a college review authored by a student, Alex Angel, who had written that *Shadowdance* "is a blend of weak instrumentation and boring songs, forming the base for musical garbage. The music is simple and unbelievably repetitive. It all sounds like background music of a terrible B movie, possibly called *If I Urinate on Your Sneakers, Will You Still Call Me?* This results in an uneven, bland sound which rendered Sam, my pet bullfrog, comatose."

Although certainly not the first, nor the last, unappreciative review that Shadowfax would receive, it had an enraging effect upon Chuck and Phil. Phil became so indignant that, strengthened by the Schnapps and galvanized to action by who knows?—latent primeval urges?—he ran over to the curb and literally ripped a parking meter out of the ground.

Chuck was astounded. "No one will ever believe this happened!"

"Yes, they will—we're takin' this back to the hotel and showin' 'em!" screamed Phil.

The problem then became how to get this unwieldy thing back to the hotel. Renting a cab was out of the question, which left skulking down back streets as their only option. After smuggling the meter into his hotel room, Phil began swinging it wildly as if it were some sort of trophy, tossing it finally onto what he thought was an empty bed—except that it wasn't. Jamii had been fast asleep until being almost decapitated by a flying parking meter.

The Windham Hill years on the road were especially fun. Shadowfax toured often with guitarists Will Ackerman, Michael

Hedges and Alex de Grassi, and by the end of each tour it became customary to play tricks on each other.

Shadowfax at Red Rocks, 1984: Chuck, Phil, G.E., Stu and Jared Stewart [l-r], courtesy of Claudia Salot-Engel

One tour-ending show happened in Philly. The band and crew arranged for the t-shirt salesgirl to speak "dirty" directly to Will through the monitors when he got up to open the show. Will didn't know if the audience could hear her, and he got so flustered he left the stage. Sound Guy Stevo had to reintroduce Will, and he barely managed to collect himself enough to walk back out and play.

Next on stage was Michael Hedges, who always stuck a piece of incense in his guitar and lit it. Stevo had managed to find a trick exploding lighter and when Michael asked for one to light the incense, Chuck handed him the trick one, which caused the incense to explode in Michael's face with a big bang. He wasn't hurt—just very surprised—and immediately plotted his revenge. So when it came to the part of the set where Shadowfax played "Shadowdance," Michael got the stage hands to switch on the strobes behind a translucent psychedelic curtain that extended the full length of the stage behind the band, lighting their instruments. Unbeknownst to the band members, Michael came out

103

and stood in front of the lamps, casting his shadow on the curtains, and "shadow-dancing" to the song. Chuck noticed about two-thirds of the way through the tune, then the whole band turned to watch Michael as he brought the house down.

Stevo helps Chuck through a sound
check, 1995, by Ray Kachatorian

Finally, it was time for the set-ending "Brown Rice." Michael had secretly picked up five pounds of brown rice, and every time G.E. sang the words "brown rice," Michael threw a handful onto the stage—a great trick until some rice got stuck in Chuck's Lyricon console, and every time he pressed a certain key it would stick. It took Stevo a long time to clean the rice out of it after that, but he claimed it was worth it for the audience's approving response.

Audience reaction was, indeed, one of the most entertaining parts about touring with Shadowfax. In the many years they performed, at least fifteen times they'd have couples come up to them before or after the shows and tell them about how Shadowfax was the only music they ever made love to. This happened one night when they were playing in the Grand Ballroom of the Wyndham Hotel in Austin and a guy came up to Chuck before the show, saying, "You've just gotta meet my wife—she loves your music so much!" The band went on, with Chuck at stage right. Sure enough, this guy and his wife had planted themselves behind one of the speakers and were sitting Indian-style, groping each other with the girl in the guy's lap. Chuck noticed first and turned to stare at them. Pretty soon the girl had her head in the guy's lap and the whole band was watching them, although they were hidden from the rest of the audience. They groped during the whole show, with Shadowfax watching them and managing to keep their composure, consummate performers such as they were!

Shadowfax in Japan, 1984: Charlie Bisharat, G.E., Chuck, Harry Andronis, Prince and Princess, Stu, Phil and Dave Lewis [l-r], courtesy of Charlie Bisharat,

The Early Winnebago Tours were otherwise highlighted by Chuck's notoriously poor sense of direction. One time, percussionist Adam Rudolph had picked up driving duty somewhere in the middle of the San Joaquin Valley, in transit from L.A. to Santa Cruz for a gig there. The Valley—known for its dense tule fog—was so enshrouded that night that we were forced to drive at a snail's pace. What should have been a three-hour trip had already taken four, and we were still stuck in the Valley.

105

After it seemed like we had been going in endless circles for a long time, Chuck decided we were not on track at all and took over the controls. We finally straggled into Santa Cruz at about two a.m. Chuck, thinking he knew what he was doing and where he was going (usually a mistake), headed the RV down a residential street, trailer full of gear in tow. Suddenly, a very big problem loomed ahead: a train trestle so low that we could not pass under it without decapitating the RV. The only other possible move was to back up through an extremely narrow, curving street—not the most pleasant prospect at that hour, but the only practical option. We ultimately did extricate ourselves from this predicament but not before awakening the entire neighborhood and acquiring a police escort.

I was so mortified when the squad car arrived that I hid in the loft of the RV, hoping no one would see me, pretending to be a kidnap victim, with a line ready in the event of my being discovered: Honestly, Officer, I've never seen these guys before in my life! They picked me up back in Bakersfield and gave me a ride!

The standing joke thereafter would become that Chuck had been lost in more cities of the world than anyone in the universe.

Fortunately, most reviewers of *Shadowdance* were considerably kinder than Alex Angel and his pet bullfrog, Sam. Leonard Feather was favorably impressed enough to write in November, 1983, that Shadowfax was "the group most representative of a new idiom aborning. It is not jazz (improvisation seemingly plays a secondary role) and despite the electronic effects, it is not rock. Forget about categories; it is new and worthy of serious study."

Equally confounded was *Billboard*, which made *Shadowdance* a Top Album Pick for the week ending August 27, 1983, while stating, "...this fusion ensemble...taps enough rock, jazz and Third

World elements to straddle more conventional commercial jazz format...they could even lure rock play."

Jazz critic for the Cal State Long Beach student newspaper Rich Spindel wrote, "Exquisitely produced, *Shadowdance* is at once immediate and accessible, yet there is much to sustain a detailed aural inspection of each chart."

Undaunted by the inability to categorize the band and their music were their audiences, who responded ecstatically to Shadowfax's records and live concerts and were prompted to write about their reactions. "Audio painting" was a phrase used by one. "I have never heard anything like it before," wrote another. "I congratulate you on a rare and beautiful piece of art."

* * *

Carnegie Hall concert posters, 1985,
courtesy of Charlie Bisharat

Although Chuck was making a concerted effort to refrain from using the band as a "star vehicle" for himself, many responses were directed particularly towards him. Chuck was beginning to discover that the connection he was making through the business activities

107

he handled for the band were resulting in the general impression that he was its leader, however ad hoc that designation might be. Journalists, agents and label executives alike were naturally gravitating towards him for information and were even referring to him as "Mr. Shadowfax"—something he never really sought but treated as another responsibility nonetheless. As Stevo put it, "Chuck was the flux. Everyone had a key part, but it was only under Chuck's direction that all the parts fit into the puzzle. Chuck was the glue; he made the machine. A lot of what he did was important to the band and to the individuals. It would have broken down long before it did were it not for him."

Unfortunately, rather than appreciating the hard work and time involved in cultivating and conducting the business affairs for the band, several of the members began chafing at Chuck's leadership, inevitably creating a rift.

Contributing to Chuck's sense of separation was the fact that he and G.E.—who had by necessity been composing most of the music for the group—were now earning song-writing royalties for their efforts, thanks to A&M Records taking over the distribution of Windham Hill and requiring the payment of "mechanicals" as part of the deal. The heretofore non-composing members now regarded song-writing as a financially lucrative endeavor, a perception that was reinforced when NBC selected "A Thousand Teardrops" to be used as background music during the '82 Winter Olympics, resulting in huge royalties. Chuck never composed music with the express purpose of making money; he wrote because the band needed material for their recordings. However, feeling left out and desirous of augmenting their incomes as well, the current non-composers decided to jump on the bandwagon. A song-writing frenzy materialized, with attention focusing on quantity rather than quality. Band members who had never composed before began submitting tunes in various states of incompletion, expecting the others to devote much of their precious rehearsal time to working them up and having tantrums if their half-baked pieces failed to make it onto future albums. As a result of being put into the positions of both band producer and composer, Chuck felt more and more isolated.

XIII

DREAMS
OF
CHILDREN

Won't you come on out, Maceo
Your mama, she be callin'

Phil Maggini, "Maceo"

I got to tag along on some of the first road trips. Chuck, ever the intrepid manager/business person/booking agent for the band, continued to arrange for a rental Winnebago to cart the guys and their equipment around. Since gig fees were still minute and Chuck was concerned about everyone making at least a few bucks, he stuck to renting one or two rooms in a motel and taking turns sleeping in the Winnebago. By the end of the road trip that was one odoriferous Winnebago!

Despite the relative discomfort of the sometimes "no-star" accommodations, in some ways those were the most fun times I ever had with the band. The interim between the first Shadowfax album, *Watercourse Way*, in 1974 and the second, *Shadowfax*, in 1982 had not been the most productive musically for most of the band members. Attitudes were now upbeat as everyone was thrilled to be making a living again at what they loved doing the most: making music. G.E. Stinson concurred that these were his fondest memories with the group as well. "We were at our closest as a band, having been reborn, and the new opportunity to play made everyone happy."

Besides the album *Shadowdance*, 1983 brought a new arrival to the Greenberg family. It was somewhere in Marin County—Cotati, possibly—that our first son was conceived. Chuck would refer to him as our "Winnebaby," since it had been "our night" for the RV. Like the other early tours, this one featured Chuck's expertise at saving money by using a Winnebago as both transportation and hotel room.

I had been hoping for a girl and had already selected a name: Elea Claire, after my mother, Eleanor Claire. Chuck, justifiably, complained about the unfairness of excluding him from the naming process, so we compromised and made a deal: if our baby were a girl, I would name her. If a boy, Chuck would be the namer. When the amniocentesis indicated a boy, Chuck began to gloat delightedly and to torture me with all sorts of monikers that were more appropriate for pets than people.

"How about 'Spot'? What about 'Skippy'?" he chortled.

Not wanting to feed his perverse satisfaction at winning the naming contest, I tried to hide my consternation—Chuck would take any negative responses to his name ideas as encouragement.

One day he came home from a rehearsal and said, "How about 'Maceo'?"

"I like that," was my immediate reply. "Where'd it come from?"

"Maceo Parker. You know, James Brown's sax player." Pretty soon, all the guys in the band were calling our unborn baby "Maceo," and even if I'd wanted to, I could not have changed his name. Maceo he was.

Chuck was a nervous, if not downright reluctant, father-to-be. Although we had been married over a year, and I had made clear my intentions as far as parenthood was concerned, he initially felt he had somehow been tricked into fatherhood.

"But, Chuck, I told you I wanted children!" My biological clock had been ticking away. Furthermore, losing my parents so early in life had created an additional need for a family.

"Yes, but does it have to be now?"

"Well, I'm thirty-four, and I'll be almost thirty-five when the baby comes.
When did you want me to do it? When I'm ninety? Besides, you were the one who said, 'Fuck the diaphragm!'"

There was a lot of sulking and recrimination at first, but eventually he came around and even began to exhibit some excitement. He also agreed to attend childbirth classes with me. Knowing his erratic schedule, I asked a longtime friend, Dallas, to accompany us to these classes to ensure that at least one of them would be present to coach me for Maceo's birth.

As irreverent as he was during our wedding, Chuck kibitzed even more at the childbirth classes, which had about eight pregnant moms and their coaches who were mostly serious and uptight, unlike us. We would be silly and laughing while rest of the class would be taking notes. This was not the most fun group of people to be with two hours a week. They needed to lighten up and have some fun.

One night when Chuck was with us the teacher had us all lie on the floor to do some relaxation exercises. This was not all that easy since it was such a little room, and with so many very large stomachs there was hardly any space to lie down, much less relax. So the teacher gave us relaxation instructions and told us how to breathe slowly and deeply. The room got really quiet and still as she turned off the light when all of a sudden Chuck called (with perfect timing), "All right, everybody—group grope!"

I laughed so hard I thought I'd pee in my pants and get thrown out of the class. It was the most fun we'd had the whole time, and it was just what the group needed. That laugh relaxed us more than any amount of deep breathing exercises could have. This was so typically Chuck—always able to relieve a tense situation with his inimitable humor.

Luckily, when it came time for Maceo to be born, Chuck was in town. On December 8, 1983, I went for a scheduled appointment with my obstetrician, Patty Robertson, who informed me that the baby's head was dropping and my cervix was still sixty percent effaced and one centimeter dilated, as it had been a week ago. I had been having occasional contractions and a heavy pelvic feeling for a while, but Patty said I still had one to two weeks to go. She wanted me to use the fetal monitor for a "non-stress test" but as there were several in line before me to use it, I decided to return the next day.

I arrived at nine a.m. to use the monitor. After being hooked up, I began massaging my nipples as instructed to stimulate contractions. After about 30 minutes Nurse Practitioner Jackie Snow checked the print-out and came into my room looking very somber. Apparently, the baby was experiencing "deceleration,"—a decrease in his heart rate following contractions—indicating stress. Jackie checked with the doctor and advised me to go to the hospital immediately for further testing. I was not surprised at this turn of events as I had noticed fluid leaking from my water bag during the past night.

Once at Santa Monica Hospital, I was told the monitor would be in use for a while and to go have lunch and return at noon. I came home, did some final packing, ate turkey salad and enlisted a very nervous Chuck to take me back to the hospital. The monitor was still busy so we waited outside the room until one p.m., when I was finally hooked up. This time I was given an IV for the purpose of administering Pitocin to stimulate contractions. It very soon became clear that there were still decelerations happening and the decision was made by Patty, who was on call now, to induce my labor.

Because all the rooms were full, I was wheeled into the Recovery Room at three p.m. where Pitocin was again administered. By now my Lamaze coach Dallas had arrived along with G. E. and Suzanne Stinson. The extra support was nice, since Chuck was long a basket case. Patty informed me there was a thirty percent chance for a C-Section due to the fact the decelerations were occurring during relatively weak contractions. She feared the umbilical cord might be wrapped around the baby's neck. I was not surprised at this development since Dallas' husband Bob, an internist, had already mentioned this and I had gotten the hysteria out of my system then.

As the Pitocin took effect my contractions became four to five minutes apart and were lasting about one minute. Dr. Patty came in to put an internal fetal monitor in place. It was an uncomfortable procedure, to say the least. Then she told me there was now a fifty percent chance for a C-Section. At about five p.m. a room was freed and I was moved into it. I was two centimeters dilated now and progressing well.

At eight p.m. the Stinsons returned with my sister Jill from the airport. By now I was three cm dilated and having contractions strong enough to require deep breathing. Dallas helped by rubbing my back during them. They still were four to five minutes apart but were now lasting a couple minutes. I alternated sides to lie on until it was determined that the decelerations were worse on my left side. I stayed on my right side after that. But so far the baby was holding his own, although the possibility of a C-Section continued to hover like an unwanted party crasher. When I opted for the bathroom over the bedpan, the internal monitor fell out necessitating its replacement. The ensuing discomfort reinforced my decision to stay in bed for the duration.

By nine p.m. I was four cm dilated and the contractions were fairly intense—like extreme menstrual cramps accompanied by an intense lower backache. I asked for medication and was given Nisentil, which enabled my relaxing somewhat between contractions and made me so spaced out I completely lost track of time. Chuck helped rub my back most of the time, joking constantly. Pretty soon the room took on a party atmosphere. The guys from Boyz Town came over. Warren, Jungle John, Phil and Ron arrived. Everyone wanted to be there for the birth of the first "Shadow-brat."

Eventually, the nurses kicked everyone out and they ended up on the front steps of Santa Monica Hospital drinking Crown Royal together. Phil was particularly moved by the experience and composed "Maceo," which would wind up being recorded for a later Shadowfax album, Too Far to Whisper. "Maceo" featured a lively soprano sax by Chuck and was one of only three songs with lyrics ever recorded by Shadowfax:

> Won't you come on out, *Muh-SAY-oh*
> Your mama, she be callin'

From there on events became a blur. At some point the contractions became one long pain, with ebb and flow but no distinct ending, just a subsiding. I had more Nisentil but the effect was imperceptible. Somewhere I began having the urge to push which at first I refused to acknowledge, thinking I wasn't far enough dilated. Soon I realized I needed to use the blowing technique to avoid pushing, but it was hard not to push. I felt all my excretory orifices evacuating.

At some point in the fog, Patty came into the room, examined me and looked excited—I was now just about fully dilated and almost ready to push. I asked for more medication, but she said an epidural would require thirty minutes to take effect which could endanger the baby, that I was doing fine with my breathing and couldn't I hold off? I said I'd try, but I was less than thrilled at the prospect of intensifying pain. She began stretching the lip of the cervix to get me from nine and a half to ten cm. Surprisingly, it didn't hurt.

Finally I was ready. They wheeled me into the Delivery Room and placed an oxygen mask on me. Jill and Dallas continued to massage my back. Fortified by the Crown Royal, Chuck returned just in time to help with the massaging. He was an excellent coach, although I think his role as photographer was more to his liking-- having a camera between himself and the copious body fluids emanating from me was more comfortable for him. He never could stand the sight of blood, real or imagined. He didn't like watching movies that were even remotely gory. He had refused to watch Platoon in the movie theater with me, and I caught him on more than one occasion hiding behind our couch to avoid such sights on TV.

Even with all my solicitous birth attendants, I was groaning from the pain and effort of trying not to push. Then Patty instructed me to take a couple of breaths, then hold back on pushing while she gave me an episiotomy. Finally I was ready to push, and I pushed with everything I had, making loud animal grunts each time. After about twenty minutes of intense pushing, I felt a *s-w-o-o-s-h* and Maceo Horner Greenberg came sliding out. He immediately peed on Patty and let out a few cries. He looked great—all pink and smooth—enough to garner a nine Apgar. The cause of the decelerations was determined not to be the cord

117

after all, but the placenta, which was calcified, probably due to my gestational hypertension and diabetes.

I held Maceo on my belly while Jill cut the umbilical cord because Chuck—ever a wuss around blood—had declined the opportunity. Then Chuck, who had hidden behind his camera during the entire event, came over and held Maceo gingerly. After a few minutes the nurses whisked our baby to the nursery to clean him up then gave him to me in the Recovery Room to nurse, which he took to readily.

* * *

Despite his initial reservations, Chuck was a caring father. He did, however, inform me that he would not be changing any diapers.

"My dad never did and I don't plan to either," he said.

"Humph," I said. "We'll see about that!"

Otherwise, he was a useful baby-sitter, except for one notable day. Maceo was about three months old, and Chuck had just returned from one of his Las Vegas jaunts with Phil and Warren. He had been up for about two days and nights gambling and rabble-rousing. When he finally returned home, I was anxious to get out of the house to do some errands.

Maceo [l]—a chip off the Old Block [r]

I had put Maceo down for a nap and told Chuck that if for some reason Maceo awoke, just to give him a bottle. I then set off for the store, only a few blocks away.

Finishing my shopping, I had been gone maybe forty-five minutes and was heading home. As I drew closer, I heard the unmistakable wail of a baby in great distress. Sure enough, it was Maceo, and by the time I reached him he was so distraught that he was livid and drenched in sweat.

When I went looking for Chuck, I found him sound asleep on our bed, snoring peacefully.

* * *

Yes, 1983 had proven to be an eventful and rewarding year for Chuck both personally and professionally, capped by Cash Box voting Shadowfax Best New Jazz Group. Billboard followed suit, naming *Shadowdance* 20th Best Jazz Album. *An Evening With Windham Hill Live*, featuring many of their solo artists, garnered third Best Compilation by Various Artists.

Chuck's presence on "Clockwork" with Alex de Grassi and "Visiting" with Will Ackerman had helped propel the success of the early Windham Hill "sampler," Live. Will had been so smitten by Chuck's contribution to "Clockwork" that he had asked him to write a Lyricon part for a tune he was working on himself. Chuck was happy to oblige, knowing that pleasing the boss was always politically correct.

I was six months pregnant with Maceo and sleeping most of the time when Will came down from San Francisco and dropped by our apartment in West L.A., where we had moved in order to escape the insane Hungarian landlord who owned the Santa Monica apartment where we were married. As I awoke from an afternoon nap, I was treated to the sounds of Chuck's lyricon wafting from our living room. He had invited Will over to collaborate on a song for Will's upcoming album. My understanding of how the lyricon was named was reinforced once again as an exquisite melody dazzled my auditory senses. I was struck by the lyrical beauty of Chuck's melody and the phenomenon of hearing something so precious right in my own home. It turned out to be the seminal version of "Visiting" that I was hearing.

Will Ackerman and Chuck, 1983, courtesy of Jerry Howell

Years later, following Chuck's death, I received an e-mail message from a man who was sending his condolences and sharing a story "which could not have been written in the book of my life without the inspiration" of Chuck. Adrian Martinez went on to say he had been in his late teens, struggling in a rock band and trying to make something of himself. It was also a time when his life was in total disarray—his older brothers had moved away from home and his mother had started dating again after her divorce. He had reached the point where he no longer knew where he was heading. His life was "in chaos," but his way of thinking, composing and directing his life would soon "change forever."

Adrian was flipping through the television channels on a warm summer morning in the streets of South Central Los Angeles where he resided at the time. It was a typical morning—birds chirping outside, his "front door wide open to whatever breeze entered" his living room, and the sound of television stations punctuating the air as he continued to look for something interesting to watch.

Ready to give up on finding a morning program, he heard a guitar player finishing up one of his music pieces. Being a guitar player himself, Adrian wanted to see why this guy thought he was good enough to be performing on TV instead of Adrian. As the guitarist finished his song, a huge crowd gave him a warm applause.

"He's pretty good," Adrian thought. "Let's see what he does next." As he set his attention to what the guitar player was saying to the audience, he heard him say, "Please welcome...Chuck Greenberg..."

It was the song titled "Visiting."

Years later, Adrian continued to be haunted by "Visiting" because, he wrote, from the moment he heard it, he "was never the same. Chuck's performance was truly overwhelming. His style, presence and display of talent was something that can't be duplicated. That day, as with many days, he brought life not only to his instruments, but to people such as myself. He inspired me—he did. I'm now a composer of film scores and flamenco ballads. I've released my own CD titled *A Moment Shared*. I have my own record label and produce other artists.

"Sadly, I was never able to tell him how he had impacted my life, but I salute Chuck and I thank him for sharing his playing with the world. I'm quite certain wherever he's at...he's just...visiting."

XIV

DISTANT
VOICES

Shadowfax is the most original and creative new electronic group of the last decade.

Leonard Feather, *Los Angeles Times*

In 1984, the band went back to Group IV to record its third Windham Hill album, *The Dreams of Children*. The lineup had changed this time. The Chicago Four decided to replace Jared Stewart, who had performed on *Shadowfax* and *Shadowdance*, with a new keyboardist. They did not have to venture far to find David Lewis, who lived only a few blocks down Santa Monica Boulevard from us Greenbergs.

Dave had performed with Ambrosia, experiencing some success in the L.A. area. Furthermore, he had the "right equipment," meaning he possessed the necessary instruments to play the kind of music Chuck, et al., had in mind. He owned a Yamaha DX7 keyboard synth and a memory moog synth—key elements that would enable the band to record and perform the complex pieces they were composing at the time.

In coming up with a title for the new album, Chuck was obviously influenced by his new fatherhood. He had entitled a lullaby-like piece featuring the lyricon "The Dreams of Children" and was so proud of this particular track that he would thereafter claim it to be his "masterpiece." It became the album title as well.

Taking an active role in all facets of record production, Chuck managed to come up with the cover artwork for *The Dreams of Children* also. We had taken a drive up the coast to Big Sur where we stopped at the Coast Gallery. Big Sur once had been the home of Henry Miller, who just so happened to be one of Chuck's favorite authors. Unbeknownst to Chuck at the time, Miller was also a gifted watercolorist whose art was on display at the Coast Gallery. As we explored the dozens of prints by Miller there, Chuck suddenly became animated.

"Hey, check this out!" he yelled to me from across the gallery.

When I walked over to see what he had discovered, I found that it was a print of a primitive-looking watercolor by Miller entitled *Childish Dream*.

To Chuck it was nothing short of serendipity—a weird déjà vu fraught with symbolism and meaning—and he just had to have it for his album cover. This proved to be easier said than done, for part of working with Windham Hill involved dealing with Art Director Anne Ackerman, Will's erstwhile wife. Anne did not take kindly to outside suggestions for cover designs. She had carefully created a classic "look" for her label that consisted of pastoral photographs and was not eager to digress from the established norm.

As persuasive as Chuck could be, he had a hard time winning Anne over on this one, particularly since she cherished her role as in-house artistic expert. Eventually, however, he prevailed by virtue of vetoing all the alternative options. I think he just wore Anne down with his thinly disguised scorn for what he dubbed the "broccoli" covers.

The Dreams of Children proved to be the most compositionally collaborative album thus far. Besides tunes penned by Chuck and

G.E—separately and together—there was one by Dave Lewis ("The Big Song") featuring his "wall of sound" synth work and an upbeat track by Phil ("Shaman Song") that had been written during a party in our West L.A. apartment living room. We couldn't fit the baby grand into the room, so Chuck used our kitchen counter bar as a stand for his electric keyboard. Phil had come to visit, spotted the keyboard, and ended up working out the melody for "Shaman Song" while the party swirled around him.

Chuck's rhythmic, catchy lyricon composition, "Another Country," which was also the leadoff track, turned out to be a hit off the record—along with G.E.'s vocal tune "What Goes Around"—receiving airplay on both rock and jazz stations. G.E. felt that The *Dreams of Children* was the band's best work, "compositionally, the most evolved and technologically proficient—we really knew what we were doing."

Critical acclaim for *The Dreams of Children* was ecstatic. BAM magazine, producer of the Bay Area Music Awards, bestowed the band with a Best Jazz Album Bammy. The trade *Performance* awarded them Jazz Breakout of 1984 from their Readers' Poll. Leonard Feather again waxed rhapsodic over it and the band's Beverly Theater concerts in L.A. of February, 1985, writing that Shadowfax "reaffirmed to an intensely receptive audience its stature as the most original and creative new electronic group of the last decade."

Cash Box called *The Dreams of Children* "heady, sweeping, world music from the guys who can make stone flutes go hand in hand with memory moogs. The ages, and genres, come together here, and while much of it is romantic and evocative, there is plenty that is powerful and muscular. A tonic for sore ears."

Down Beat's John Diliberto added, "Shadowfax is a composer's band, with meticulously wrought compositions that are played (and recorded) with an unerring precision." The *Pittsburgh Press* wrote that Shadowfax "has found a way to move ahead with its distinctive sound without moving away from it," claiming that *The Dreams of Children* was the band's best, and had special praise for Chuck. "If there is one dominant voice in Shadowfax, however, it is that of Greenberg's woodwinds. Whether on soprano sax, flute, or the mysterious-sounding lyricon, Greenberg spins out lines of fluid melody. *The Dreams of Children* shows that Shadowfax is a band that's not growing older, but growing better."

* * *

As thoughts of the band turned to touring once again, another change in personnel became necessary. Jamii Szmadzinski was a brilliant violinist who had contributed inestimably to the early success of the band, both on record and on stage. His animated solos during live performances always elicited excitement and were perennial crowd-pleasers. Furthermore, he and Chuck were good friends who related personally as well as musically. They had met while working on a soundtrack at Group IV. However, Jamii had developed a serious drug problem which was interfering with his ability to maintain his commitments to the band and was causing extreme volatility in his personality. On one occasion he had gotten so wired that he had taken an expensive bow and flung it across a hotel room, shattering it.

On another occasion, he became so upset with Chuck when Chuck attempted to discuss Jamii's problem that he tried to throttle Chuck. The last straw was when Jamii failed to show up for a photo shoot which had been rescheduled just for him, after he missed the first one, offering what Chuck considered to be the lame excuse of "traffic." Truly heartbroken, Chuck would say it was the hardest thing he'd ever had to do, but he had no choice—Jamii had become a liability and had to go.

Finding a replacement for Jamii wasn't easy. As in any band, it was important for players to mesh both musically and personally. With a big '84 summer tour looming, Shadowfax eventually settled upon Steven Kindler, who came from his home in S.F. and stayed with us while the band rehearsed the tunes that they would be performing on the road. Kindler sported an impressive background, having played with the likes of Jeff Beck and John McLaughlin's Mahavishnu Orchestra. While his chops were indisputable, once out on the road he presented an egocentric persona both on and off stage, regarding Shadowfax as more or less a "backup band" for himself, which didn't sit too well with the rest of the group.

By summer's end Kindler had completely worn out his welcome and was asked to leave. Naturally, the odious task of firing him was bestowed upon Chuck, who was further disgusted when Kindler, pleading for his job, wrapped his arms around Chuck's knees as if he were begging for his life.

The tour with Kindler was memorable in other ways as well. In Oklahoma City the band found itself hotel mates with some Republican conventioneers. Chuck—always interested in politics—had gotten drunk in the hotel lounge and begun insulting every Republican he could find. When he finally returned to his room and passed out, some of the other guys thought it would be funny to stack every available piece of furniture on top of Chuck to the point that if he had moved an eyelash, a mountain of chairs would have come crashing down on his head. Fortunately, someone took pity on him and removed the furniture towering over him while he slept.

G.E. was in a funk the whole tour from news of the death of Oregon's Colin Walcott, who had been one of his idols, which made him even less tolerant of Kindler's megalomaniacal antics.

Despite the interpersonal squabbles, the band looked and sounded as meticulous and professional as always, a fact that can

127

be seen in the live video produced at what was once Doc Severinson's club in Oklahoma City.

* * *

The summer of 1985 saw the reissue of *Watercourse Way*, Shadowfax's fourth album for Windham Hill. Released to little fanfare, it generated renewed interest and sales, if mainly for its historical perspective on the band's music. Chuck, as usual, oversaw all the reissue production details and although compact discs were making their entrance onto the market, he was adamant about pressing only records and tapes. He felt that even with remixing and remastering, the sound quality of *Watercourse Way* was still not up to par, and its inherent inferiority would only be highlighted on a CD. As an added plus, since there was very little studio time involved, *Watercourse Way* was relatively inexpensive to produce, meaning that royalties would begin accruing almost immediately.

Those reviewers who published their comments about *Watercourse Way* indicated a range of reactions from surprise to infatuation. The Washington Post wrote that *Watercourse Way* "represents the storm before the lull. Right from the start, beginning with 'The Shape of a Word' and G.E. Stinson's tortured guitar solos, and continuing until the art-rockish climax of the last track, 'Song for my Brother,' it's obvious that this is not just another musical sedative from the popular West Coast label Windham Hill."

The *San Diego Daily Aztec* reviewer wrote that "while their live performances are stupendous, their spontaneity has not always transferred well in vinyl. However, *Watercourse Way* may be their best album, with all the energy and enthusiasm of a live performance captured."

Thus, 1985 had seen Shadowfax returning to the road to support *The Dreams of Children* and the reissue of *Watercourse*

Way. Management responsibilities had eased up somewhat on Chuck now that they had an agency (Variety Artists) to do the booking for the band and could finally afford to hire a tour bus and equipment truck. Variety Artists head agent Bob Engel was impressed with Chuck's business abilities. "Every band wishes they had a Chuck Greenberg," he said. "Chuck was a more than capable businessman and an exemplary artist—something you rarely find in one person."

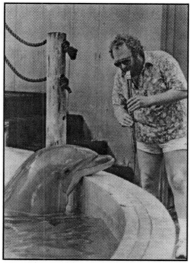

Chuck plays for Alfie, 1985

It seemed that humans were not the only ones entranced by Shadowfax's music. Cindy Ward, the dolphin trainer at Six Flags Over Georgia in Atlanta, had written a letter detailing the fondness of her charges Alfie and Schooner for Shadowfax. She said that she had been playing several albums, but when she got to Shadowfax, "the animals stopped working and stuck their heads way out of the water to listen. I'm familiar with this position, because they do it when I'm talking to them. They have pinholes on the sides of their heads, and have to raise themselves way up out of the water to hear—and damn if they didn't do it for your music!" She went on to invite the band to come by and play with the dolphins the next time they were in Atlanta. They did just that, turning the event into a cute sound bite for CNN. Sure enough, when Chuck played his lyricon, Alfie and Schooner swam over and hooked their heads over the edge of the pool, listening intently.

There were other memorable tours as well. Variety Artists booked a gig that turned out to be a gambling boat in Fort Lauderdale. The boat would cruise three miles out to sea, where gambling restrictions did not apply, and entertain its customers with live concerts. They had to do two shows on the boat because the concert room couldn't hold everyone at once. Complicating things was the fact that the union stevedores were technically required to move the equipment from dock to boat at a cost of several thousand dollars. The promoter decided it would be cheaper to hire a local crew—the only problem being how to sneak past the stevedores, who would not take kindly to being cheated out of their work. They had to get all the gear into the boat at four a.m. so the stevedores, who came on at five, wouldn't find out.

They soon discovered there was no way to get the stuff off the truck except by opening the hold and driving the semi right onto the boat. Now they had to get the gear up five or six floors, using an elevator that only held five people. They ended up unloading it piece by piece—a slow process that worked okay until they got to the mixing consoles, which were too big for the elevator. So they had to take them back down the ramp to the dock, across the gangplank, and past the stevedores, who figured out immediately what was going on.

Chuck performing at Disneyland in 1986

The shows went great, and by ten p.m. the boat had returned to dock. The road crew managed to get everything back down to the hold and onto the truck except the mixing consoles, which had to be taken back across the gangplank. The stevedores were waiting for them on the dock, arms across their chests, shoulder to shoulder. They had pulled the gangplank and refused to put it back until the promoter coughed up $5000. He had no choice at this point. It ended up costing him twice what it would have, not to mention all the extra work and time, if he'd just let the stevedores do it in the first place.

* * *

With each successive Windham Hill album, Shadowfax had attempted to more closely replicate the drive and energy of their live concerts, without alienating the growing and devoted audience they had so carefully cultivated with their recordings. When it came time to go back into the studio for their fourth go-round (fifth release including the reissued *Watercourse Way*), Chuck was feeling conflicting pressures as the band's producer.

131

On the one hand, the label powers wanted a variation on what had already been successfully accomplished—based on the premise "If it ain't broke, don't fix it."

On the other hand, Chuck was being pressured by his band mates to allow them more freedom, especially in terms of contributing compositionally. While the band had been set up essentially as a democracy, with each member theoretically having equal say artistically, Chuck's position as interface between the label and the band had made him the ultimate decision-maker. Although it might be more democratic to allow equal representation compositionally, the fact remained that not all songwriters were equally gifted. Chuck found himself in the unenviable position of passing judgment on a submitted tune by either rejecting it or spending an inordinate amount of valuable time trying to make it acceptable and recordable.

In fact, Chuck's business duties for the band had become so time-consuming that he had not been able to do much composing himself. So, when it came time to record, Chuck was able to contribute only one tune, "Streetnoise," to *Too Far to Whisper*, the new album. He had also come up with a lovely lyricon melody for another tune, but had gotten stuck before finishing it. After submitting it to G.E. and Phil, they were able to collaborate on the first and only three-way credited tune by Shadowfax, "Ritual," which would prove to be one of the most popular tunes the band would record, even though it was never performed live. A private environmental group, The Nature Conservancy, selected it in 1992 to be used on a soundtrack for one of their promotional videos, *A Stitch in Time*, which featured a clip about the rain forest.

"Ritual" must have generated strong rain forest images in other listeners as well, for one fan felt compelled to write that he had recently completed a painting based on "Ritual." The four-panel, fourteen-foot-long work was the result of three months work by himself, his wife and his daughter. Since hearing "Ritual" evoked "such a strong, clear image of a rain forest I had no choice but to create this painting. My wife and daughter translated the music into musical notation which I then converted to color values and shapes. The painting was the main work at my Master's of Art Exhibition at the University of Wisconsin, Madison."

The rest of the new album consisted of compositions by Stinson, Maggini, Lewis, new violinist Bisharat and Nevitt. As an interesting change of pace, two of the tunes featured vocals: G.E.'s "What Goes Around" and Phil's "Maceo." The album took its name from the other G.E. tune, "Too Far to Whisper."

Recorded and mixed at Group IV, *Too Far to Whisper* was released in 1986. Joining the band's nucleus of four in the studio were percussion guru Emil Richards again, Adam Rudolph on tabla, Morris Dollison (the Chicago blues buddy who had recorded with them under the moniker Cash McCall and lent vocals on "Maceo"), violinist Charlie Bisharat (hired to replace Steve Kindler) and—adding some spatial-sounding background vocals—Haralambi A, aka recording engineer and sometime Shadowfax Sound Guy Harry Andronis.

Shadowfax in '85: G.E., Stu, Chuck, Phil, Dave Lewis and
Charlie Bisharat [l-r], courtesy of Sam Emerson/Windham Hill Records

Charlie injected a new enthusiasm and youthful flair into the band. A recent grad of USC, where he had once considered pre-medicine, Charlie—like Jamii before him—added considerable virtuosic talent to Shadowfax. He also contributed the lovely composition "Road to Hanna" to *Too Far to Whisper*.

Although the reviews for Too Far to Whisper were favorable and lauded its obvious musical diversity, the whole recording process had been enervating and disappointing for Chuck. While having a "democracy" was all well and good for the individual band members, they were incapable of forming any sort of consensus on their own—someone ultimately had to make the final decisions. As producer, Chuck felt he was that "someone." This meant he was in charge of determining which tunes would make the "cut" and be recorded out of the many that were being brought in to rehearsal. As far as Chuck was concerned, it didn't matter how many of your own tunes made it onto the record—if it didn't sell well, you weren't going to be raking in those coveted mechanical royalties. In other words, twelve or fifty percent of zero was still zero.

In order for an album to sell well, Chuck believed there had to be well-crafted tunes. However, the rancorous rank and file refused to recognize or respect Chuck's judgment and critical role. Some seemed to look at song writing as something anyone could do, and Chuck felt that the others perceived that he was being selfish about restricting their individual contributions. In attempting to please and appease everyone else, he failed to please himself, leaving him with a sense of disillusionment. He vowed never to produce Shadowfax again.

The studio was not the only place where internal rivalries and competitions were brewing. Concerts were being turned into forums for one-upmanship, manifested by on-stage "volume wars." In an attempt to be heard above everyone else, one guy would turn up his amp, then someone else would do the same thing, and by the end of the show it was so painfully loud that some in the audience complained or ran defensively from the room, hands clapped over their ears.

Nevertheless, *Too Far to Whisper* gained airplay and generated decent sales, if not to the same levels of *Shadowfax*, *Shadowdance* and *The Dreams of Children*. "What Goes Around" received the most attention on radio, emboldening its composer, G.E., to bring more songs with lyrics to the band.

G.E. was inspired by the South African political situation at the time and had written a song called "Ashes and Dust" reflecting his passion. While Chuck and Phil did not feel the material was right for the band to record, they did make concessions to G.E. as far as playing the song live. This would lead to a fateful turning point in the destiny of Shadowfax.

XV

TWO-HEADED
ALARM
CLOCK

The main thing is to prize who you are and to have the courage to live. And this, Chuck did. He was a brave soul.

Mark Bernstein, from a letter

Chuck and Shadowfax were on a European road tour when I found out I was pregnant with twins. I had gone in for a routine third-month checkup in June of 1983, when my obstetrician measured my ballooning abdomen and announced that I was "quite large" for my due date of late December.

"Do you have a history of fibroids?" she asked.

"No, but I have a history of twins," I replied. "I have a fraternal twin sister." With that I was immediately dispatched for a sonogram, which confirmed my suspicion. I reacted with cautious excitement—on one hand, I had really wanted twins with my first pregnancy, but on the other hand, I hadn't really wanted more than two children altogether.

I decided to withhold this bit of news from Chuck for a while, at least until I felt certain he wouldn't freak out. As much as he loved Maceo, he was not thrilled at the thought of adding more children to the family. He had become accustomed to the idea of my latest pregnancy only after much encouragement from the other guys in the band like Charlie Bisharat, who said, "That's great, Chuck! Now Maceo will have a playmate!" But two playmates? I was afraid this might push the already precarious Chuck—always stressed out when he was on the road—over the edge.

The beginning of the tour had not gone well. The band had arrived in Madrid and promptly had their wallets stolen by the cab driver on the way to their hotel from the airport. Some of the guys were bitching about what they considered to be poor accommodations, and cliques had developed with behind-back whispering. As usual, Chuck found himself in the unenviable position of tour manager and resident rabbi. But things seemed to pick up when they got to Montreaux, where they were treated like stars. I was dying to tell Chuck about the twins, so when he called me from the Côte d'Azur sounding relaxed for the first time since he'd been gone, I made the announcement.

Chuck and Charlie on the Côte d'Azur, 1985,
courtesy of Charlie Bisharat

"Oh, my God!" he said, sounding like I'd just informed him of a death in the family. "First we had one, now we're having two...our family is increasing geometrically! I feel like a...a...a *Mexican*."

Needless to say, it was not the reaction I'd hoped for. "Oh, come on, Chuck" I said. "It's not that bad. Twins are fun. You'll see." I was trying to bolster myself as well as him. In fact, I remembered my mother telling me just how difficult my twin sister Jill and I really were, especially during their first year of infancy. But I had always enjoyed being a twin; it made me feel special.

"Why'd you have to tell me now?" He sounded ready to cry. "Just when I was starting to have fun."

"Well, if you're going to pout about it, I'll talk to you later," I said. I was not in the mood for his whining. In fact, I entertained a momentary fantasy of wrapping the phone cord around his neck—an inclination that told me it was time to end the conversation. I decided to let Charlie work on him some more, figuring Chuck would come around eventually. And he did. By the time he got home a few weeks later, he seemed to feel better about the whole idea. In fact, he acted like it was all his doing, as if twins were a reflection of his superior masculinity. I let him delude himself. Whatever it took to get him interested and positive was fine with me. However, I could have done without his first comment to me when I picked him up at LAX.

"You look like a beach ball with eyes! Are you sure it's only twins?"

"Gee, thanks, Chuck. I really needed that." It was bad enough that strangers were staring at me and saying, "Any day now, eh?" when I was only six months along.

By November my stomach protruded so much I could hardly move. I was therefore relieved when Dr. Patty put me on bed rest for the duration of my pregnancy.

"We've found that's the best way to keep twins from coming prematurely," she said. "And by the way, it's not uncommon for the second twin to have problems necessitating a C-section."

"You mean, I could have the first one by natural birth and then end up having a C-section with the second?" I didn't like the sound of this at all.

"That's exactly what I mean," she said.

"Well, forget that! Just give me a C-section right from the start!" It was agreed that I would be scheduled to enter the hospital two weeks before my due date of December 30.

On December 11, I went to the doctor's office for a "non-stress test" to see how the twins' hearts were functioning, as I had done with Maceo. When the nurse weighed me, I tried not looking at the scale, but it didn't matter. She called out "two-oh-eight" to the clerk recording my vitals. Horrors! I'd gained sixty pounds! "Don't worry," she said. "You'll lose twenty when they're born." I did not find this prediction at all comforting. What about the remaining forty?

As I considered my ballooning proportions, the nurse stuck me in a tiny room about the size of a phone booth, strapped some monitors around my belly and told me to relax. "Yeah, right," I grumbled. "You try relaxing when there are sixty pounds of excess weight pressing on your bladder."

"Well, we need to get you to stimulate contractions to see how they affect the twins," she said.

"How do we do that?" I asked.

"By massaging your nipples," she said. I stared at her for a moment, attempting to judge whether this was her idea of a joke. It was not. "Can I get you something to drink in the meantime?"

"No, but do you have any porno movies I can watch to get myself in the mood?" Now it was her turn to stare back at me before she chuckled slightly.

"Oh, don't worry. You'll do just fine. Just go to it," she said in her cheery nurse's tone.

I looked down at my swollen belly with the straps hugging it. I could see the veins spidering out from my navel that was stretched so tautly it looked like it might rupture. Lifting my XXL t-shirt so that my breasts were exposed, I grasped my nipples and lightly rubbed them. At first I felt silly and self-conscious, but it was not an altogether unpleasant sensation. In fact, it felt rather nice.

A few minutes later, just as I was beginning to really get into my nipple massage, the nurse stuck her head through the "privacy" curtain and said, "Good job. Go home, pack and meet Dr. Patty at the hospital.

"What? You mean it's time for the C-section?"

"Yes. The babies are having heart decelerations and it's time to get them out."

Gian and Gregory Greenberg came into the world later that evening.

The Two-Headed Alarm Clock at band practice
on Halloween, 1994, courtesy of Jean Collins

* * *

Although Chuck was present during the birth of the twins, he resumed touring soon thereafter. Being home alone with two babies and a toddler proved to be a daunting task, so I followed the best advice ever given me and hired a young girl to help out. Esther would arrive in the morning, help feed the twins, and take Maceo out to the park while they napped. I would nap when they did, since getting enough sleep became a personal quest. Even though the twins were good night sleepers, they rarely became hungry at the same time, which meant I was up for multiple feedings. I never got more than a few hours sleep at a stretch for the first few months, giving new meaning to the term "sleep deprivation"—a situation that became compounded when Gian contracted pneumonia at three weeks.

Chuck had just returned from the road and was out grocery shopping on a January Saturday morning when I woke from a nap. I knew immediately something was wrong—I never awakened on my own; the crying of one or both of the "two-headed alarm clock" always got me up. But it was eerily quiet this time as I hurried to the living room where the twins' bassinets had been set up. Looking down at Gian, I gasped in horror to see his skin a pale blue.

I picked him up and rushed him into the bathroom as I'd been instructed by the pediatrician, starting the hot water in the shower with my free hand to get some steam going.

"Prop him up and take his temperature," Dr. Wasson had said when I'd called the day before, worried about Gian's difficulty breathing. I took his temperature now; it was normal. But Gian didn't look normal. In fact, he looked really bad. His breathing was shallow and slow. Where's Chuck? What should I do?

As the panic began to rise in my throat, I called a good doctor friend and described the situation. By the time I said the word "blue," he said, "Go to the ER now!"

I dashed upstairs, still in my pajamas, to drop Greg off with my neighbors. Just as I was loading Gian into his car seat, Chuck drove up with the groceries. As soon as he saw Gian's limp little body, he ordered me into the car and said, "Don't put him in the car seat. You'll be able to give him mouth-to-mouth resuscitation easier if he's in your lap, in case he stops breathing." This was something I hadn't considered, and I was grateful to have Chuck home and taking charge.

By now I was petrified with fear. Still in my pajamas, I cradled Gian and pleaded with him to keep breathing while Chuck sped down the center dividing line of Santa Monica Boulevard toward the hospital. When we arrived, the nurse took one look at Gian and whisked him away without bothering with forms or checking us in.

Once Gian was stabilized, some of the ER staff came out to the waiting room to tell us his diagnosis: pneumonia.

"But I don't understand," I said. "I kept taking his temperature like Dr. Wasson told me and he was always normal."

"But don't you know?" said the nurse. "Babies this young aren't developed enough to get a fever."

My panic turned to rage. "What?" I said, trying not to scream. "Then why the hell did the doctor tell me to take his temperature? Shouldn't the most expensive yuppie pediatrician in Santa Monica know this?" The nurse just shrugged and looked away.

Later that day they moved Gian to the Pediatric Unit at UCLA Medical Center where he stayed for three days, and I got to find out what it was like getting up for only one twin during the night. It was the most sleep I'd had in a month, and I needed it. It was the closest I've ever come to losing a child, but I gained respect for Chuck, who handled the situation with amazing aplomb.

"I've always wanted to go ninety-five on Santa Monica Boulevard," he enjoyed telling his friends later. After all, crawling along at a snail's pace on the traffic-snarled street was the norm.

"In fact, I was hoping to get pulled over by a cop on our way to the hospital. I thought a police escort would be really cool." In typical Chuck fashion, he had managed to keep his cool and even joke about our ordeal. In so doing, he had defused much of the tension. I, on the other hand, went home from the emergency room and downed three Valiums. It had been the most frightening experience of my life. But it would have been so much worse if Chuck had not shared it with me.

Chuck's longtime friend Mark Bernstein noted the same attribute in Chuck's personality, saying he believed that "Chuck was something of a lightning rod for other people's momentary crises. He was a good listener but a better friend, in that he listened in a way that suggested that this momentary crisis was just that, momentary, and that what mattered was something else.

"Perhaps I dwell on this because in this aspect I was different from Chuck. I am prone to believe that whatever were the pending disasters imagined in my past—however often they did not in fact come to pass, or weren't disasters when they did, or proved to be useful disasters—nonetheless the disaster I face at the moment is a real one. And, of course, it's not. It's not the main thing. The main thing is to prize who you are and to have the courage to live. And this, Chuck did. He was a brave soul."

XVI

A
PAUSE
IN
THE
RAIN

Word has it that my family was started in the room Chuck
used as his personal home studio. It's a magical place, that
house in Paradise Valley!

Russ Davis, from a letter

With the addition of Gian and Greg, the Greenberg
apartment on West Colby in West L.A—once considered
spacious because of its two large bedrooms and two
bathrooms—became a cramped clutter of baby paraphernalia and
musical instruments. Part of its initial appeal when we first moved
in had been that the owners had promised not to raise our rent as
long as I performed as building manager. When they decided to
increase it after all, we thought it might be prudent to start
looking elsewhere. At the price of $650 a month, plus a stipend of
$150 that I earned from showing vacancies and collecting the rent
from the other eleven units, the apartment had been a good deal.

But now that the landlords wanted $800 a month, it was losing much of its luster. Fortunately, we had been able to amass a little nest egg, thanks to an unexpected windfall.

Chuck's composition "A Thousand Teardrops" had been selected as background music during the 1982 Winter Olympics. NBC formerly programmed athlete profiles called "Up Close and Personal" and played Chuck's tune enough times during them that six months later there arrived two huge checks from Broadcast Music Incorporated (BMI), one of two companies that collect and dispense the royalties for all performed music.

I was pregnant with Maceo when the first check covering the artist portion arrived. It was so much larger than any other BMI distribution we'd ever received that I wondered if a mistake had been made. When Chuck called from the road, I said, "Do you think they put the decimal point in the wrong place? What should I do?"

"Cash it!" he said, ever the prudent one when it came to financial issues. Two weeks later, the music publisher portion arrived. Because Chuck had wisely formed his own publishing company—Greenshadow Music—for his compositions, he retained the rights to all his publishing as well as artist, or composer, royalties. He had seen what happened to composers who—as part of their deals with recording labels—had signed away their publishing rights. It had allowed one of the strangest kinds of music business ironies to take place: the purchase by Paul McCartney of Buddy Holly's catalogue and, in turn, the purchase by Michael Jackson of the Beatles' catalogue.

As we contemplated possible applications for our newfound wealth, the idea of escaping our crowded quarters began percolating. There seemed to be no particular reason to remain in L. A. even if we could afford its pricey housing. Armed with the belief that Chuck could pursue his music career from virtually anywhere, we decided to head north to look for a suitable place to live. Furthermore, Chuck still harbored a primitivistic, back-to-nature hippie ideal from the early seventies when he had purchased some riverside acreage in Wisconsin with three friends: Phil Maggini, Bill Johnston and Jeff Paris.

According to Jeff, not long after he and Chuck began to hang out together, Chuck introduced him to an extraordinary woman named Ursula. Ursula had bought a farm in northern Wisconsin and was getting ready to move there. She invited them to visit, which they did. On their first trip into Hurley, Wisconsin, they stopped for a burger at a local diner.

"The native telegraph was up and running," said Jeff. "Soon we were surrounded by a group of curious teenagers who'd never seen the likes of us before. Chuck, hair and beard a maelstrom in red, his barrel chest thrust out, drew most of the attention. He was a true exotic in their eyes. Not only did he look like a crazed hippie but he was a rock musician too!"

Now, in the early seventies Hurley was a cultural backwater. As one of the boys said in answer to Chuck's question about what they did to entertain themselves: "We drink beer and fuck. Sometimes we go out to the dump and watch the bears feed on garbage." Some years later they found that boy's answer to be true. Curious about the bears, a group of them found themselves on the access road to the dump. In every bush, on every tree leading into the dump, hung women's underwear and condoms.

Chuck and Jeff became enamored of northern Wisconsin on that first visit. So much so that before they drove back to Illinois, they had Ursula's real estate agent show them some properties. They'd asked to see properties with houses on them, but didn't see anything they liked. Finally, the agent suggested they check out a piece of river property. It had no standing buildings, but it had three-quarters of a mile of river frontage along seventy-seven acres of meadow and woods. Once they saw it, they knew they had

147

to have it. The price was only a hundred dollars an acre, but at that time, those were big numbers to them.

On the drive back, Chuck and Jeff spun scenarios on how they could buy the property. Halfway down Wisconsin, they realized that between them they'd never be able to raise the funds quickly enough. But by the time they reached Illinois, they'd worked things out. They would find land partners. Chuck had several friends who might be interested and Jeff thought he had a few friends who might go for owning land in Wisconsin. "Within hours of our return," said Jeff, "we were both evangelizing the glories of northern Wisconsin to our friends."

Not too many days later, they made the trek north with Phil and Bill. "Prepped beforehand, the real estate agent took us on the same tour of disappointing properties, ending with the river frontage. We signed the contract and made a down payment the same day."

"We're land magnates now," someone said as he surveyed his new domain.

"More like land maggots," Chuck joked, pointing at himself and his scruffy little group cavorting in the meadow. And land maggots they remained, despite a changing roster of owners over the years.

Land Maggots: Bill Johnston, Chuck, Jeff Paris
and Phil, [l-r], courtesy of Jeff Paris

But Wisconsin was not a practical base for someone with both a burgeoning music career that required a proximity to the big city and a wife accustomed to the ideal California climate.

So, with dreams of a more rural lifestyle dancing in our heads, Chuck and I ventured north, stopping at the first spot that was sufficiently tree-laden, safe and cheap. In Paradise Valley we found such a place where we could exchange the reptiles of Hollywood for far less pretentious alligator lizards and gopher snakes.

Our search yielded five and a half wooded acres backing up against rugged mountains, seven minutes from town—with reputedly good schools and safe parks—and only a forty-minute drive to the airport. Here we could strip away the façade that usually stands between us humans and the universe. Here we could create our own universe.

We found paradise. Well, technically it's called Paradise Valley, an apt name for a place of such ethereality as to reinforce faith in the divine. It is obvious that whoever selected the valley's title felt the same way, despite the Spanish moniker given to the city: Atascadero—and road: Cenegal. Translated, it means we now lived on Swamp Street in Mudhole City. But it is far lovelier than it sounds.

Situated at the central, eastern edge of the Santa Lucias—the "crown jewel" of the southern Coast Ranges—Paradise Valley is a sun-drenched cleft separating parallel, north-south ridges that unite at both ends of a small valley carved eons ago by Graves Creek, a tributary of the Salinas River. Our home is at the southwestern tip of the valley, nestled among the lace-lichen-laden oaks, bay laurel, mountain mahogany, ceanothus and toyon which typify this classically Central Coast California oak woodland.

We chose our property for its abundance of trees and wildlife, and for the nameless seasonal creek that rushes past our home as

149

soon as the first storms arrive, singing its sweet lullaby so long as the heavens cooperate to sustain it, bolstering its bounty of frogs and newts, winding its way to an eventual marriage with Graves Creek. This No-name Creek is one of many similar streams dissecting the valley when they awaken from their dormancy in late fall, attracting deer, raccoon, fox, opossum, puma, bobcat, turkey and quail, all of whom seem to be singing the poetry of Robinson Jeffers: "Be glad for summer is dead and the sky/Turns over to darkness, good storms, few guests, glad rivers."

—And for the mountains "which seem to reach to the heavens," as early explorer Juan Rodriguez Cabrillo noted in 1542, upon spying the mighty Santa Lucias for the first time. I had always wished to live in a place where I might go for a hike without having to get in my car first. Here in Paradise Valley I found such a place. To exit my back door is to enter my own private wilderness.

—And for the sky, in all its permutations from daybreak to alpenglow and beyond. Yes, the sky, which with its Milky Way presents an evening display as awe-inspiring as that of any other, heretofore unseen by us until our arrival in Paradise Valley, where there are fewer city lights to dilute its spectral spectacle. Here we witness Orion, who ascends late above the hills, as though weary and drained by his nightly climbs. And the Crab Nebula in the constellation Taurus, a star in the process of exploding, whose light from its explosion first reached the earth in 1054. It was a supernova then—so bright it shone in the daytime.

—And for the rocks: huge serpentinite outcroppings that tumble down the hillside and into No-name Creek. Rocks that sing when the rains come.

The natural beauty of Paradise Valley provided much inspiration for Chuck. The seeds for many of his compositions germinated while he gazed across the varying vistas—a place more reminiscent of his beloved Wisconsin with its climatic extremes than the

Southern California we left behind. He also enjoyed practicing his chops on the variety of wind instruments he played—flutes, saxophones and lyricons—positioned on our deck facing the woods. It was here that he wrote my favorite of all, "A Pause in the Rain."

Chuck enjoyed composing, living and walking among the mountains and trees of Paradise Valley, so long as he didn't have to work too hard at getting there. One day I forced him to hike up the deer trail that leads to the top of the mountain behind our home. After huffing and puffing for about thirty minutes, we stopped to gaze out over the verdant hills.

"Now, wasn't that worth it?" I said.

"Yes," he replied, "but if you could just airlift me here and let me walk down it would be better." Still, he did appreciate nature, however oddly he may have expressed it, as in that early composition he wrote for Eko-Eko, "Sensory Overload."

Celebrating Hanukkah, 1989: Greg, Gian, Maceo
and Chuck [l-r], by the author

Yes, Chuck could be moved to song by a beautiful view. I'll never forget the first time we drove up the road from Lihue to Hanalei in Kauai. As we rounded the last bend before being greeted by a vista of mountains plummeting to the bay, Chuck suddenly broke out into a rendition of "Bali Hai" that was saved from potential corniness by his hilarious falsetto, complete with vibrato. Our friend, Nancy, who was traveling with us, and I immediately cracked up, giggling the rest of the way to Princeville. It was only one of many times that Chuck made me laugh so hard I got tears in my eyes.

Even though it was mainly scales or the repetitious construction of a melody Chuck might be working out, there was always something soothing about his silvery sylvan songs drifting from our home. Others must have concurred, for following his death, from one of our neighbors came this message: "When we go out in the afternoon and sit on our deck, we will think of Chuck. We will miss his music filling our little valley. We will listen for him in the wind and the sounds of nature." And sometimes—when the breeze picks up just so at sunset, lofting the lyrical lamentations of the towhees through the canyons of the Santa Lucias, and within the pauses of the rain—I hear him once again.

XVII

WE
USED
TO
LAUGH

I remembered seeing a dog once with only three legs, and he seemed to be getting along all right, so we decided to forge ahead.

Phil Maggini

Following the release of *Too Far to Whisper* on Windham Hill Records, Shadowfax entered another period of transition. Chuck had produced all of the albums for Windham Hill, and he and G.E. had composed most of the material. Each deal had been between Chuck and Windham Hill, with Chuck distributing artist royalties to the rest of the band members. Mechanical, or songwriter, royalties had never been paid by Windham Hill until a distribution deal with A & M Records forced Windham Hill to pay mechanicals on all their recorded music. This meant that Chuck and G.E., as the primary songwriters for the band, were now earning additional royalties for their compositions. When the band members who previously had not done much writing discovered they could be augmenting their income even more by working up some tunes, a frenzy of composing took place.

It had become Chuck's job, as producer, to select the tracks for each record, but others in the band thought he was unable to be objective since his own compositions were being considered as well. Chuck ultimately decided he would have to relinquish producing duties because the other musicians were giving him such a hard time about his choice of what to record.

At the same time, several of the band members mistrusted Windham Hill and wanted to label-shop to find a better deal. After all, Windham Hill had contracted directly with Chuck, not Shadowfax. Some of the guys seemed suspicious that Chuck had set things up for his personal benefit rather than that of the band. Of course, nothing was further from Chuck's mind than exploiting the band. If he were only in it for himself, he would have recorded a solo album back in 1981 rather than putting Shadowfax back together again. But the other band members were itching to find out if they could get a better deal elsewhere. And so, against Chuck's better judgment, the band decided to leave Windham Hill and sign a deal with Capitol Records, which offered a far more lucrative contract and seemed willing to launch Shadowfax into the Big Time.

The opportunity to go to Capitol presented a situation similar to the one at Windham Hill. As with Will Ackerman, the band had a very enthusiastic head of A&R in the person of Tom Whalley, who arranged for a very profitable agreement with them based on his perception of what Shadowfax was all about. He had been following the band through the Windham Hill years and felt he could take them to the next level—a goal which had become more elusive as years went by. The band members had grown frustrated with Windham Hill's disinterest in their ideas, including the release of a live record, which they thought would help present a side of the band never captured in the studio.

Right around this time, in 1987, Variety Artists got the band booked at the Universal Amphitheater—considered a coup and major step up for Shadowfax. It was an important gig for the band because it would mark the first time that the Capitol people would be seeing the band live, so it was a showcase of sorts. Bobby McFerrin—who had just come out with "Don't Worry, Be Happy"—opened for the sold out show, and when the band came on the air was electric with excitement. All was going well; Shadowfax was playing great. Then, towards the end of their set, they went into a new tune by G.E. that had lyrics, something never before included in the live Shadowfax repertoire, excepting "Brown Rice." Even though Chuck had warned me they were working up new material, I was unprepared for the overwhelming negative response I felt and observed as I listened to the opening bars of this song. So I did the usual thing when the band went into one of those rare tunes I didn't like: I got up and went to the restroom.

In the meantime, the band segued into yet another new G.E. song that I found equally unappealing. As I attempted to return to my seat from the Universal restroom, there were so many people pouring from the hall to the exits that I had to fight my way back to my seat like a salmon swimming upstream. I guessed they weren't enjoying the new stuff either. To make matters worse, the band had committed a cardinal performance sin by placing this new material at the end of the set. This meant that if the audience didn't like the new tunes, they would leave the concert with negative thoughts about the whole show foremost in their minds and thus feel cheated. On the other hand, debuting new material near the beginning of a set gives the band a chance to recoup some excitement by the end, in the event that the new stuff is not well received. I learned later that this placement of his new material was also G.E.'s idea. It proved disastrous, and Chuck knew it.

Backstage at Universal after the concert a meeting occurred between Chuck, Phil, Whalley, and Bobby Engel of Variety Artists—booking agent and one-time manager for the band—in which Chuck and Bobby worked hard to satisfy a dubious Whalley that those new vocal songs didn't represent a change in musical direction. At this point, Whalley needed some assurance; the deal was in jeopardy. So Chuck and Phil made it clear that G.E.'s South African protest songs would not be included on the new recording without serious revision. G.E. interpreted this as a "kangaroo court" situation, and it created a huge rift between him and the band.

Even so, Phil helped G.E. on his songs in an effort to try to make them all they could be. They worked diligently on the vocals, wanting to be sure that if it became apparent that the songs would not make it on a record, it could never be said that they didn't try as hard as they could to realize them.

"In hindsight," Phil said, "to insist on such a 'left turn' in musical direction at such a pivotal moment was an error in judgment." He believed they owed Tom Whalley the same consideration that they had given Will Ackerman, and "to present this 'surprise' in the form of music that was a radical departure from what he was expecting in his first live concert experience of Shadowfax only amplified his confusion over signing us."

In the end, the decision was made not to include G.E.'s protest songs on the new album.

Recording *Folk Songs for a Nuclear Village* was therefore tortuous for Chuck, even though he was not technically the producer this time. Capitol had hired a guy who spent most of his studio time on the phone or eating carrots, and whose main function seemed to be keeping the band from killing each other while objectively deciding which tunes would make the final cut.

Watching someone so inept make $50,000 doing what Chuck had always done for free drove him nuts.

Capitol Records promo shot, 1989: [l-r]
Phil, Stu, Chuck, Charlie, Dave, G.E.

Although the venture with Capitol Records ultimately proved to be ill fated, critical and popular plaudits for Shadowfax continued. As always, requests to use the music for a variety of purposes persisted. One source for these requests was the dance and choreography community exploring interesting instrumental music for their programs. When it came to the attention of the band members that the avant-garde dance troupe Momix was choreographing Shadowfax recordings, an ambitious idea began formulating, particularly after viewing a live Momix performance.

Under the leadership of Moses Pendleton, a founder of the daring, groundbreaking modern dance troupe Pilobilus in the early '70s, Momix had cultivated a loyal following of dance aficionados, despite the fact that it, like Shadowfax, had always defied categorization. Known for its onstage antics as well as unusual assortment of props—including skis, stilts and a giant rotating spherical contraption—Momix seemed like the perfect visual accompaniment to Shadowfax's distinctive music.

157

After meeting with Moses, Chuck, G.E. and Phil decided to include him and his choreography in the music video that Capitol arranged to promote *Folksongs*. The success of the video for the Chuck composition "Firewalker" combined with a developing camaraderie between dancers and musicians led to a tour featuring both groups. The Momix/Shadowfax collaboration in the summer of '89 was thus an aesthetic marvel—but a financial disaster.

Shadowfax in 1988 music video: Phil, Stu, Chuck,
Dave, Charlie and G.E., [l-r]

Many of those fortunate enough to attend—including myself—commented that these were the best concerts they'd ever seen. The first part of each performance showcased one to four dancers performing amazing feats of strength and agility with the band onstage but behind a translucent, backlit curtain. The "ski routine" always brought the house down. In it, two dancers facing each other on skis would rise from lying prostrate on their backs without lifting their feet or skis off the ground—a feat demanding extraordinary concentration and athletic ability.

After several numbers with a curtain separating the band from the dancers, there would be an intermission followed by another set with Shadowfax alone.

Because of the number of performers and amount of equipment involved, the tour was a logistical nightmare with such a high overhead that sellout shows were required in order to simply break even. Banking on attracting dance fans as well as music fans, the band hired publicity agents to get the word out to both communities, but some audiences were confused—the performances were so untraditional that dance reviewers didn't seem to know what to make of them and as a result, often panned them. Because of this confusion, few tickets were sold to the dance community.

Publicity art for 1989 tour

Dancer nudity was a problem for others, especially in the South. When the promoters at Wolf Trap in Virginia got wind of the one nude number, they forced its removal from the show under threat of cancellation. Other venues banned Momix outright from performing. The camaraderie between the dancers and musicians became more strained as money got even tighter midway through the tour and accommodations became less deluxe as a result. Chuck was disappointed that Moses, after performing in the video and expressing enthusiasm for the venture at first, never joined the tour.

159

Then, at the end of the tour during a show at the Luther Burbank Center in Sonoma, the unthinkable occurred: the dancer who performed on two-yard-high stilts during the last number had a stilt break under him, causing him to fall and break his leg. Consummate performer that he was, he made the accident appear to be a part of the act and managed to drag himself offstage. Only a few of us who had seen the routine before knew that anything was amiss.

To make matters worse, the tour manager—an old friend of the band's from Chicago—resumed his heroin habit while on the road, which interfered considerably with his supervision of the band's affairs. There were several times when he would be too high to take care of backstage business, forcing Chuck to take care of collecting the night's earnings. As a result, he came home broke and disgusted. It was the first time the band had ever lost money on the road—an event Chuck had worked arduously to avoid through the years. But circumstances had necessitated the hiring of others less adept than he at managing the band's affairs, and so the band was, quite literally, paying the price. The net result was an exacerbation of internal strife within Shadowfax.

XVIII

WHEEL
OF
DREAMS

I should have just shut up and played my drums.
Stu Nevitt

Despite, or perhaps because of, the mounting tensions within the band, touring often had an equalizing effect on everyone. Being on the road seemed to bring out the best and/or worst in those involved. Although the stress of being an entity as opposed to a disparate group of individuals was often heightened by touring, cohesion was essential for the type of ensemble band that Shadowfax personified. For them, it was like being married to six guys at the same time without the ability to "kiss and make up"—at least, not with these guys. As a result, anything that contributed to the unity of the band was a welcome addition. And what could be more unifying than life-sized, anatomically correct, inflatable female doll?

One night after a gig, Phil ended up at the club owner's place. When his host promptly crashed, Phil was stranded. Looking around the house for some way to escape his predicament, Phil discovered "Loretta" and knew he had to have her. The problem of how to get her and himself back to the hotel presented itself. Getting a cab wasn't too difficult, but getting back to his room unnoticed was. But somehow he managed.

Loretta was an instantaneous hit with the band. Everyone became extremely solicitous of her, making sure that she was adequately, if not decently, attired. She would acquire a new wardrobe at each destination on the tour and had quite an extensive lingerie collection at one point. One wag contributed gaffer's tape for a set of garter belts. As Phil said, "Loretta was a unifying thing for the band. She gave everyone a project, like the tree of life."

Stu's attraction to Loretta was based on his perception that her mouth formed a "voiceless, pleading, ohhhhh."

Eventually, it became apparent that some unnamed persons were beginning to take Loretta just a little too seriously. They were paying a little too much attention to her current fashion. She had taken up residence in the Lizard Lounge part of the Winnebago but was exhibiting signs of wear and tear. Gaffer's tape soon had to function as more than holding up Loretta's stockings—it had to patch some of the leaks to which she was succumbing.

The Lizard Lounge was sort of a road version of Boyz Town. Its walls had been papered with porno pictures in a sort of X-rated collage, enhanced by stage lighting gels that gave it a permanently green, otherworldly glow. Within this ambiance Loretta found a home.

Sadly, Loretta was beginning to resemble an old tire. She ultimately became so disgusting that she was relegated to the roadies in a demonstration that even the music business has a pecking order. Once doomed to the roadie truck, Loretta was never to be seen again, typical of all relegations to roadiedom. The roadie truck was like the Bermuda Triangle—once something disappeared into its recesses, it vanished forever.

* * *

Loretta and the equalizing nature of road tours notwithstanding, communication among the band members had disintegrated so badly that when *Folksongs for a Nuclear Village* was nominated for a Grammy for Best New Age Album of 1988, G.E. refused to attend the awards ceremony. But, oh, what a party he missed! Highlights for me included the haunting, exquisitely lovely ballad sung by Sarah Vaughn during the Awards Ceremony, meeting Bonnie Raitt at one of the many parties afterwards, and boogying the night away to the Neville Brothers. Chuck's most memorable experience was meeting Pharaoh Sanders at the Grammy Nominee Reception the night before the Awards Ceremony.

When we returned to the Biltmore after the reception, Chuck wanted to be prepared in the event the band won and decided to write an acceptance speech.

"I want to have something written down so that I won't get up to the podium and look like an idiot," he said. It took him only a few minutes to write on a piece of paper taken from the Biltmore pad in our room:

> All of us in Shadowfax have tried to create music with quality and integrity. We felt if we stayed true to our musical vision, we would find an audience. It has been a long road from where this band started to this stage and we would like to thank everyone who made the journey possible. And we thank all of you for honoring us with this Grammy Award.

Save for the absence of G.E., there was little visible evidence at the Grammys of the intense intra-band turmoil that was tearing Shadowfax apart. Then—in yet another blow to its fragile stability—as the result of an internal shakeup at Capitol typical of the record industry, the band found itself without a label. Grammy notwithstanding, Shadowfax was summarily dumped. What the guys discovered was that it takes the same amount of energy and money for a label to promote, for example, Michael Jackson as it does to promote Shadowfax, but the returns are much greater on Jackson. So big labels look for big sales and big stars. Despite its success, Shadowfax was considered small change at Capitol.

Accepting their Grammys in 1989: Phil, Stu, Chuck,
Charlie and Dave [l-r], courtesy of NARAS

Now on non-speaking terms with Chuck as an expression of his sense of betrayal at Chuck's failure to understand and support his protest songs, G.E. became more and more negative and aloof. He felt the band was stagnating creatively, repeating itself by recording the same music over and over. He kept pressuring the band members to introduce new elements and influences into their compositions but was considered a pain in the ass and overly critical as a result. The members of Shadowfax had stopped communicating with one another.

Chuck was crushed. He felt personally rejected by G.E. and believed that G.E.'s continued negative presence had become a threat to the viability of the band. Chuck began having episodes of insomnia, knowing that the decision to separate from G.E. would have to be made or the band would not go on.

That Shadowfax had always been essentially a quartet made this decision even more difficult. The addition of personnel could accommodate performances and flesh out musical ideas, but as long as the four of them were at its core, they could be fairly confident that whatever came about musically would be true to their collective vision. Over time, contributions of added personnel were integrated into their soundscape, and more often than not, they enhanced that vision. "For example," Phil said, "the marriage of Charlie's violin with Chuck's lyricon often enriched the timbre and ultimately the accessibility of Chuck's lovely melodies." But the problems with G.E. and "other personal dilemmas caused a fracturing of the collaborative vision that had always furthered our process before."

When Capitol dropped Shadowfax, the band's momentum screeched to a halt. The thought that a label could so easily dump a Grammy winner had never crossed their minds. They went scrambling for a new label, ending up on Private Music, now a part of the BMG conglomerate that eventually absorbed Windham Hill as well. Shadowfax released one album on Private Music entitled *The Odd Get Even*. It would be the last recording with G.E. Stinson. In a telling moment, Chuck entitled his contribution to the album "We Used to Laugh."

Not since having to fire Jamii Szmadzinski had Chuck faced such a difficult task in terms of personnel management. After all, Chuck and G.E. had been friends—very close friends—for fifteen years. Chuck valued G.E.'s creative abilities and often praised him for being the best composer in the band. But G.E. was committed to writing protest songs with lyrics, the antithesis of the innovative instrumental sound Chuck had been carefully cultivating with Shadowfax. G.E. was struggling to find a way to continue to participate as well as pull the band into much needed fresh air. He had, to a degree, already disenfranchised himself, however, and his individual writing effort was pulling him further and further away from anything previously recognizable as Shadowfax.

Chuck finally solved the G.E. problem when the opportunity arose, once again, to change labels. The deal with Private Music that had produced one album, *The Odd Get Even*, had soured. By mutual agreement, new contracts with EarthBeat! would be signed leaving G.E. out of the "mix." Losing his friend and band mate had been an unendurable ordeal for Chuck, the psychic cost of which was clinical depression. Chuck began having bouts of insomnia.

Of course, it was difficult for G.E. as well, and he now takes full responsibility for his part in it. "I withdrew from the relationship completely," he said, "which was very detrimental to the band."

Stu acknowledged the part he played in the breakdown as well. "I wish I had, to paraphrase Frank Zappa, just shut up and played my drums," he said. He claimed that the most damage he did, however, was not taking responsibility for his marijuana addiction and diabetic health care. "One of the things that really impressed me about Chuck was that he was once as big a pothead as I was but managed to give it up for the sake of Shadowfax. After he moved to L.A. he stopped smoking pot, and that's when he really started getting his life and music business chops together. I'm now on an insulin pump and my health has never been better, but I still haven't come to terms with my addiction. My irresponsibility has led me to where I am now."

Part of the problem for Stu was that there was also "a lot of outside influences that came into play as we started climbing the musical food chain. Some of these were real, some were paranoid delusions." Stu had played once with a great pedal steel player in Chicago named François D'Lux (Richard Lux), who had told him that there were two kinds of band members: lead stars and rhythm pukes. "Although we were never made to feel that way by G.E. or Chuck, I think that both Phil and I were made to feel like that by some music business people. We felt some of the label people would have been happier with a Chuck and G.E. duo. I didn't deal with that very well. Subconsciously, I took it out on Chuck and felt an outside producer would give us a more 'pop' sound with the rhythm section a little more prominent. Like I said before, I should have just 'shut up and played my drums.'"

Stu regrets that he also spent "too much time trying to become a drum star like the guys I idolized. Chuck and G.E. were always encouraging Phil and me to write for the band, but I didn't write songs for a long time because I knew I wasn't even near their league as far as composing. The first tune of mine that we recorded, 'Slim Limbs Akimbo,' came out way better and much different than I had envisioned. Chuck, G.E. and Emil Richards did a masterful job of arranging and producing that." Stu admitted that by making sure everyone in the band was represented with tunes, the writing gene pool became diluted, "but by then the band's biggest strength, the creative and business sense of G.E. and Chuck combined, had eroded badly."

"G.E.'s leaving greatly saddened me," said Phil. "The quartet was no more, and to me it was questionable whether to continue or not with the project, but then I remembered seeing a dog once with only three legs, and he seemed to be getting along all right, so we decided to forge ahead.

"I'm happy we can now all count ourselves as friends after so much drama. Chuck would have wanted it that way. Life is too short, as they say. That, regrettably, and to my profound dismay, is his message to us all."

167

XIX

DARKER
THAN
MIDNIGHT

The music business is a cruel and shallow money trench, a long plastic hallway where thieves and pimps run free, and good men die like dogs. There's also a negative side.

Hunter S. Thompson

Birthing an album was not unlike a ritualistic courtship/marriage/family thing for Chuck. In the beginning of the creative process, he would doodle around for a while on his winds and keyboards until something caught his fancy, melody-wise. Or sometimes it would be a rhythm created on his synth that would captivate him. Whatever, once he got something down that he liked, he would rhapsodize about it ad nauseam (the wooing) then, eventually, ask my opinion. I learned through the years to answer very carefully. If I were too enthusiastic, he would scoff, "You're just saying that." On the other hand, if I weren't at least as enamored of a tune as he, well, I just didn't have the "ears" to appreciate good music.

Once he was head-over-heels with a new piece, Chuck would obsess over it, fine-tuning to get it just right. This part of the process could take days, or even weeks, and sometimes he still wasn't satisfied. That's when I knew the "honeymoon" was over. Frustrated and full of self-recriminations, he would rant about how he couldn't write anymore and would be better off in some menial job.

As Chuck reached a low point in the musical birthing process, he would usually "call in the troops" for help. He enjoyed writing with G.E. and often commented about how he was the most accomplished composer of the group. In the beginning this had led to many fine collaborations on the early albums, including "Wheel of Dreams," "Watercourse Way," "Ariki," "Distant Voices," "Ritual" (also with Phil) and "Petite Aubade," which went on to be included on the first *Winter Solstice* album, earning a Gold Record in the process. Later it would be young Armen Chakmakian who provided just the right collaborative magic with Chuck.

Sometimes, half-finished tunes might gestate for a while before suddenly exploding like a phoenix from the ashes/tapes. Many tunes evolved that Chuck liked but knew were not Shadowfax material. These he set aside for future solo projects. Much of *From a Blue Planet* developed this way.

Once the darlings of alternative radio disc jockeys in their heyday of the '80s, Shadowfax had been challenged to survive the vicissitudes of commercial '90s radio programming, whose dj-less format became a mass marketing tool as never before. The music of Shadowfax never did fit neatly into a "genre." However, radio programmers insisted on categorizing the music. If it could not be categorized, it couldn't be played on most radio shows. And, as any recording artist can tell you, without airplay, it's virtually impossible to "move units."

Chuck took advantage of the lull in gig bookings and lack of a recording contract with the band to pursue his first solo project, *From a Blue Planet*. By 1990, he had accumulated an album's worth of material that he had deemed inappropriate for the band or unwanted by the other members but nevertheless worthy of recording. A bright, funky lyricon piece became the second cut on side two and acquired its title following a visit to the Greenberg household by Alex de Grassi. Alex had been working on his own material while staying in the downstairs studio of our home. The first morning he came upstairs on musician time—around noon—looking a bit bleary-eyed and haggard.

"How was it for you, Alex?" I said. "Did you sleep okay?"

"It was fine," he replied, "except for the two-headed alarm clock that got me up at dawn." He was referring to our now five-year-old twins, Gian and Greg, who were used to rising early and would chase each other around the house before breakfast. The childless Alex had not figured on such an early wake-up call created by the pounding of their footsteps above his room. Chuck was immediately struck by the phrase and decided to use it for the funky song title on his new album.

Alex also contributed guitar work on several pieces, including "The Secret of Time" and "Almost a Dream." Bassist Phil and violinist Charlie Bisharat were the only Shadowfax members who played on *From a Blue Planet*, which was released in 1991 by Gold Castle Records, a label owned by Danny Goldberg who had also taken up managing Shadowfax. Danny impressed Chuck with his sincerity and honesty like no other music executive had before.

What Chuck didn't know at the time was that Gold Castle had never paid a cent in royalties to its artists. Although reviews for *From a Blue Planet* were favorable and Chuck considered it his finest effort, Gold Castle went bankrupt and never paid royalties beyond the advance Chuck received. When Chuck discovered he

171

was once again getting stiffed on a record, he was furious—not so much at Goldberg as at himself for trusting Goldberg. But Chuck managed to make the best of a bad situation by offering to accept the 20,000 tapes and CDs Gold Castle had in stock in lieu of suing them for royalties owed. Goldberg agreed to the terms, and before long, hundreds of boxes began arriving at our house.

Even so, Chuck remained bitter about the experience for a long time. So bitter that when we saw Goldberg at the Grammys a few years later, haggling with an usher about changing his seats—they had placed Goldberg in the back of the Shrine
Auditorium's orchestra section among the rest of us peons, instead of up front with the celebs—Chuck was delighted at Goldberg's obvious upset.

Phil remembered another time when he and Chuck went out to grab a bite at Louise's on Ventura Boulevard in Sherman Oaks. As they stood at the bar drinking wine, who should walk in but Goldberg. Chuck—ever the King of Schmooze—went right over and shot the shit with him for a few minutes as Phil muttered expletives under his breath. When Chuck came back to join Phil, he commented that they had exchanged pleasantries, and although the encounter was tense, they had smiles on their faces when done. Phil said it was a lesson in maintaining bridges that he never forgot.

And Goldberg never forgot Chuck for his grace in handling the Gold Castle debacle. After Chuck's death he sent a ten-thousand-dollar check to me and my sons with a letter which said, "Chuck was unbelievably kind and gracious to me during the Castle Records period which was a very costly and embarrassing business failure for me that was the low point of my career. There was no other artist who had the kind of personal sensitivity he had to me. I never felt I really earned the friendship he showed me but I certainly appreciated it."

How odd that, although I listen to our local NPR station only occasionally, I found myself hearing a recap of the 2000 Grammys and how winning one does not ensure wealth. The music mogul being interviewed was none other than Danny Goldberg. He was speaking philosophically about being canned from his latest record company executive job—he has headed Mercury Records, Atlantic Records, Warner Brothers Records and most recently Artemis Records— sounding not the least perturbed, knowing that in the true tradition of the music biz, he would soon find himself recycled into another CEO job. True to form, he popped up again on Court T. V.'s Catherine Crier Live in April, 2005, touting his latest endeavor: CEO of the liberal talk radio network Air America Radio. Such is the entertainment world, which has its own form of karmic entropy.

* * *

Others concurred with Goldberg about what it was like doing business with Chuck. I think this is because for all his lacking a sense of physical direction, Chuck more than compensated with a profound sense of spiritual direction. Moral issues were never a dilemma for him: he always recognized the right ethical choices, even if they meant personal loss. "After all," he would say, "I have to look at myself in the mirror the next morning." For this reason, he was trusted implicitly by everyone, including record company executives.

Chuck had actually been honing his business skills for a long time. Jeff Paris, a friend from their former college days at Prairie State College in Illinois during the late '60s and fellow "land maggot," recalled how he and Chuck came up with a plan for the first Earth Day.

Jeff and Chuck had been relaxing in Haskell House, a converted residence serving as the office for the college newspaper, of

173

which Jeff was the editor. They enjoyed hanging out in the office whenever they ditched classes, and to help himself think, Chuck pulled out his flute and began improvising. Jeff lay down on the floor and fell asleep, lulled by Chuck's melodious notes. When he woke up, the room had filled with people who'd heard the music. An accidental Pied Piper, Chuck had drawn in the people they needed to help them come up with an Earth Day event.

After some brainstorming, they decided to do an anti-pollution movie. They had no funds to do it with, but they could all lay hands on eight-millimeter movie cameras. Before the meeting broke up, Chuck designated himself the moneyman and left.

A couple of days later, Chuck called Jeff and said he'd figured out how to raise the money. He'd gotten hold of a student senate rulebook and therein found the solution. He'd discovered that any campus club with a faculty sponsor and at least three members serving as club officers was entitled to $125 of the student senate's money. Chuck reasoned that if they formed five or six clubs, they could all belong to the different clubs, but in different capacities as club officers or members. The key was in getting sympathetic faculty sponsors to play along with the gag and to get their clubs recognized at the next senate meeting. If they missed that meeting, it would be too late.

Chuck wasn't interested in carrying through on the mundane details, so Jeff took up that part. They managed to get their bogus clubs recognized and pooled the money to buy film and pay for processing. Chuck directed the movie and worked one of the cameras. He also directed the post-production editing as well as organizing the music and time-synching the audiotape. The twenty-minute film, which depicted a world bereft of trees and wildlife and the impact this might have on humans, debuted on Earth Day and over the course of the day was seen by more than two thousand people.

When they'd completed the editing of their movie *Ugliness Kills*, they were ready to do a soundtrack. The entire movie crew wanted to participate and they made arrangements to use some high-end audio equipment owned by the brother of the star of the movie. They all piled into a Volkswagen bus filled with stacks of records, musical instruments, slide projectors, and various pieces of audio gear. It was late in the evening when they left to get the taping equipment.

About halfway to their destination, the driver pointed out that a squad car had been following them for the last mile. It had been tailing them closely and wouldn't allow any cars to get between it and them. There was a sudden blur of activity as they all consumed whatever drugs they happened to be carrying. Once the drugs were ingested, they breathed a sigh of relief until one of the group blurted out that he'd brought along stolen audiovisual equipment.

While they were digesting that bit of news along with the drugs, the flashers on the squad car came on and they ended up being detained in a deserted parking lot. Within minutes they were surrounded by a collection of local, county, and state police. None of them would tell why they'd stopped the VW van. The would-be filmmakers were ordered to stay in the van but to leave all the doors open. They sat like that for quite some time, scared, cold, and blitzed on a variety of drugs.

"I'm bored!" Chuck complained. "Let's have a sing-a-long!" He launched into "Michael Row Your Boat Ashore," a song Jeff knew Chuck absolutely hated. Giggling like nervous schoolgirls, they all joined in. The half-dozen or so cops looked tense for a few moments as guitars were twanged and various musical instruments began appearing from bags and pockets, but then they relaxed and began to laugh as the serenade went on.

Halfway through "Kumbaya," they found out why they'd been stopped. A very pissed-off state trooper screeched into the parking lot and stomped over to the van. "These aren't the guys," he said, turning on his heels and leaving.

"It turned out," said Jeff, "that some criminal types in a van just like ours had tried to kill him with a shotgun during a traffic stop. That night, anyone unlucky enough to own a red VW van had been stopped and surrounded by cops. Within minutes we were on our way again, in search of the nearest restroom now that the drugs had worked their way through our systems."

* * *

Years later, Windham Hill Records opened an office in L.A. with Paula Jeffries in charge of promotion. She and Chuck became instant and permanent friends. "He was the big brother I never had," Paula said. When she first met Chuck, she knew she could trust him as both a friend and business associate. "Of all the artists I had come into contact with, he was the most professional and understanding. He knew how to make the 'machine' work. He pushed through, made things happen and did it all in a way that was totally cool—everyone could have fun. And, he was supportive of me as a human being. When I thought I'd lost my friends forever, he was there."

Paula was amazed at how well Chuck understood the business. "If he got upset about something, it would usually have to do with interfering with his music-making and turning people on to it. He was successful because of his sincerity—he never stopped thinking about his music—twenty-four hours a day." Chuck often stayed at Paula's house while he was recording in L.A. after our family had moved away, and he "always had something funny to say, no matter how disillusioned or tired he might be from the day's events. One time he returned home and I asked him, 'So, Chuck, how was your day?' He replied, 'It was long—but at least it was long.' It became a standing joke in our house, with 'long' being substituted with any other adjective we wanted."

Other music execs concurred with how easy it was to work with Chuck. He created such an endearing persona that everyone loved to hear from him and welcomed his phone calls. I don't know how he did it, but I certainly wish I'd paid more attention.

After Chuck died, Brad Pressman of Sonic Images Records said that Chuck touched people both socially and in business with his music. "Chuck and I spoke about life, liberty and the pursuit of high record sales and critical acclaim. He seemed to have two trains of thought—his family and his music. He spoke daily of both with genuine love and emotion." Furthermore, Chuck was able to point people in the right direction when they went astray. With Brad, it was "a case of the A&R guy having less experience than the musician, and the musician usually won."

This "warm and fuzzy" feeling was not necessarily mutual. Prudently, Chuck made sure he had a contract for any dealings with record companies, and used the legal expertise of Steven Lowy to ensure that he got the best deal possible. In the beginning, Windham Hill was not used to negotiating with someone so tenacious as Chuck, particularly an artist. In fact, no artist had ever thrown a lawyer at them before. Prior to Shadowfax, artists were offered standard contracts whose terms they could accept if they wanted to record or reject, meaning no recording deal. Windham Hill had managed to do well for itself partly because its contracts had avoided payment of mechanical royalties. Steven Lowy demanded and eventually received mechanical royalties for the band which greatly augmented the incomes of those who composed their music.

Not that having a contract with Shadowfax's last label, Sonic Images, mattered one iota: it still screwed the band. Aside from one payment of mechanical royalties from the original shipment following release of the *Live* album, Sonic Images never sent even one statement, let alone a check. And yet, label exec Brad Pressman acknowledged that sales have been brisk. If truth be told, Windham Hill, for all its shortcomings, was the only label Chuck worked with that sent statements and royalty checks on time and in conformance with contractual requirements.

* * *

Besides airplay difficulties, Shadowfax was once again going through personnel transition in the early '90s. Charlie Bisharat, the energetic, highly talented violinist in his early twenties who had more than compensated for the void created when Jamii Szmadzinski left, had abruptly abandoned the band following the release of *The Odd Get Even*. Coming from a classically trained background, he had had the virtuosic chops to perform to the high expectations of The Chicago Four, and his Middle Eastern good looks enhanced their stage presence as well. He had become an adept showman, jumping into the audience with his violin on occasion, and performing "face-off" duets with Chuck on stage.

Charlie opted for a series of better-paying gigs with whatever New Age flavor-of-the-month offered the best fees. Although he remained on friendly terms with Charlie, Chuck was hurt by his defection. He had difficulty understanding how any right-minded musician could prefer playing the drivel that he felt Charlie was doing as part of the backup bands for Yanni, Kitaro and John Tesh—even if it meant more money. In Chuck's eyes, Charlie had prostituted himself. Of course, Charlie was not the only musician ever to do so. Chuck knew he couldn't expect others to take the "vow of poverty" required for working with a band that refused to commercialize itself. Still, Chuck had thought Charlie was different.

Keyboardist Dave Lewis had lasted longer than Charlie, but he was eventually let go when substance abuse interfered with his performing and ultimately proved insurmountable. The last straw was a California gig where Dave literally forgot what he was playing—an occurrence that was becoming all too frequent, and it was worsening. Chuck took the opportunity of a lapsed recording contract with Private Music to part ways with Dave.

The Odd Get Even on Private Music had featured a fine collaborative effort from the band, yielding my all-time favorite Shadowfax tune, "A Pause in the Rain." The day Chuck arrived home with a preview of this piece after spending several weeks in the studio rehearsing for the new album, I was awe struck and wanted to hear it over and over, enchanted by its lovely soprano sax melody bridged with the lyricon.

However, just when Chuck thought he'd dealt with the most unprofessional recording label ever—Private Music—along came EarthBeat! Records. A subsidiary of the children's label Music for Little People, EarthBeat! was attempting to become known with a catalog of "world music." Although well meaning, EarthBeat! did not appear to have the slightest clue how to cultivate artists or create fine recordings. They did, however, manage to release two acclaimed Shadowfax albums, *Esperanto* and *Magic Theater*—the former garnering a Grammy nomination for Best New Age Album in 1993.

Through one-time Shadowfax Road Manager Jonathan Collins, Chuck met and hired keyboardist Armen Chakmakian to replace Dave Lewis. Armen remembered the first time Chuck arrived at his house wearing the James Brown mask he had created from a record cover photo of "The Hardest Working Man in Show Biz," which Chuck and I and the rest of our krewe had worn copies of during a San Luis Obispo Mardi Gras parade. Chuck had displayed his mask at the first meeting he'd had with the EarthBeat! heads, an act which broke the ice during what had begun as a strenuously serious conference.

Mardi Gras krewe '92:
Chuck is back right

Armen proved to have an engaging stage presence, meshing compatibly with Stu and Phil as well as Chuck. He also became a prolific writing partner for Chuck, filling the void when G.E. left the band. Armen and Chuck penned several tunes together— "Neither Here Nor There," "Moonskater," "Imaginary Islands," "Secret Gathering," "Ebony Wind," "Night Passage" and "Baker's Dozen"—for the *Esperanto* and *Magic Theater* albums. They also collaborated with Stu on *Magic Theater* with "Hey! Your Hat's on Backwards" and "How Much Does Zimbabwe?" Furthermore, it was through Armen that two new, young musicians entered the fold: Ray Yslas and Andy Abad, who added percussion and guitars, respectively. Chuck, Stu and Phil referred to them as "The Kids" because of their youth and inexperience. In fact, Chuck liked to joke that Armen, Andy and Ray should pay him for all the recording and touring "lessons" they learned with Shadowfax. Their presence infused the band with new life and their ethnicity and instruments added even more diversity to a band already known for its eclecticism, a trait that was especially highlighted on stage. Each newcomer came from a culturally diverse background and brought a varied collection of instruments and sounds to the band. Peruvian-born Andy had recently finished up college at USC and contributed on guitars and the *charango*, a South American stringed instrument. Also a Latino, Ray played a variety of percussion instruments, including African drums, *timbales*, *shekere*, congas and a box-shaped drum named appropriately *cajon*. Armen's expertise on keyboards allowed the band to play songs they'd never performed live before. It was thrilling to hear "A Pause in the Rain" finally come alive, literally. After years of attempts at regrouping following the loss of G.E. and Charlie, Shadowfax had once again jelled.

Wearing their Grammy nominee medals: [l-r] Phil, Armen, Stu, and Chuck, 1993, courtesy of NARAS

Shadowfax had always been a "musician's band" whose talents as performing artists transcended even their remarkable recordings. For this reason, Chuck had long wished to record a "live" album, but, due to the negative commercial appeal of most live albums, all the labels including EarthBeat! passed on his proposal. Thus it was that in 1994 Chuck found himself once again label-shopping, this time looking for one that would not shy away from a live album

. As clueless as EarthBeat! had been—for example, the spine of the CD cover insert for *Magic Theater* was printed upside down— Sonic Images was even worse. Besides failing to provide us with record sales statements since the release of the live album, they demonstrated just how inept they were by giving Chuck a beautiful table with an image of the album's cover printed on top, then asking him to "share" it with the rest of the band. When Chuck pointed out the logistic difficulties—it had cost us $150 just to have it shipped from L.A. to San Luis Obispo—of such a request, they suggested having him keep it for a month or so, then sending it to another band member who would do likewise until it had "rotated" through the entire band. Ever the pragmatist, Chuck persuaded them to make more tables instead.

Shadowfax in 1994: Chuck, Ramon Yslas, Phil, Armen
Chakmakian, Stu and Andy Abad [l-r], by Ray Kachatorian

Whatever they may have lacked in professional acumen, however, Sonic Images made up for in enthusiasm for the live recording. With Chuck once again producing, the band made plans to perform and record five gigs in January of 1995 at a club called Palookaville in Santa Cruz, California. From these gigs they would cull the best tracks and use them for both audio and video recordings.

Chuck in Kauai, 1989

XX

NO
LONG
GOODBYES

Looking at the night sky
you'll see the light of
hundreds of stars...
some of these
died hundreds of years ago
and
we still see their light
proof of
life after death

Robit Hairman

The Channel Islands repose just a few miles off California's Central Coast, but such are their remoteness that they may as well be on another planet. Chuck would pass Santa Cruz Island—the largest and most visible of the chain—often during his frequent trips from our home in San Luis Obispo County to Los Angeles. It appears as an alluring jewel in the ocean as one cruises Highway 101, the coastal artery that connects Northern to Southern California. The shortcut San Marcos Pass through the Santa Barbara Mountains yields a spectacular view of Santa Cruz, along with the other Channel Islands—a shimmering chain of peaks jutting from the teal blue Pacific, beckoning to be explored, yet keeping those who would do so at bay with their moat-like, perilous surrounding sea.

The public owns the eastern tenth of Santa Cruz Island, which has been designated a part of the Channel Islands National Park, along with the other six uninhabited islands. While the harbors are accessible by boat, one must be invited by the Nature Conservancy to visit the interior regions. Chuck and I visited Santa Cruz Island in 1994 as guests of the Conservancy, which has owned the westerly nine-tenths of the 61,600-acre island since 1987, when the land's former owner, Dr. Carey Stanton, died and willed it—through his Santa Cruz Island Foundation—to the Conservancy.

The Conservancy had used the Shadowfax tune "Ritual" in a soundtrack for one of its conservation videos, A Stitch in Time. In return for the favor, the NC invited our family to stay at any one of its holdings across the country. Chuck had chosen Santa Cruz Island in part because of its proximity to our home and also due to its mysterious presence—a place easily seen but not so readily understood.

Because the goal of the Nature Conservancy is to preserve the island and return it to its original pristine state, public access is limited. Permits must be obtained before docking and no dogs are allowed due to their destructive habits and the diseases they pass to native wildlife. A few times a year, the NC sponsors special events that bring visitors on day trips. Otherwise, the only regular human inhabitants are the caretakers of the old Stanton ranch and an assortment of students and research scientists who are drawn by the island's unique geological, ecological and archaeological circumstances.

Although Chuck and I had ferried to the more southerly Santa Catalina Island—the only other privately owned of the Channel

Islands—several times, we had never traveled to Santa Cruz Island until 1994. We had a great time. The caretakers of the main property, which includes the well-preserved ranch, were consummate hosts, responding with warmth to our family, showing us all over the island by Jeep, cooking delicious meals for us and allowing us to bring along my aged uncle and aunt. My uncle Ned had flown over Santa Cruz Island many times during his stint as a Navy pilot torpedoing Japanese subs during W.W. II, and he had retained his naturalist's curiosity about it for many years.

Chuck relaxing on Santa Cruz Island in 1994

As guests of honor, Chuck and I were placed in the antique-filled master bedroom that had once belonged to the Stanton family. We were treated and felt like royalty, and immediately fell in love with the peace and magic of the place. Chuck relaxed as never before on vacation. He needed this break from the otherwise ubiquitous telephone.

In his inimitable way, Chuck managed to charm our hosts so much that they invited us to return to the island over Labor Day weekend in 1995. We jumped at the chance to return. We were both feeling stressed out—I from finishing up requirements for my teaching credential, and he from the production of his second solo project. He had begun this new project in collaboration with Armen following the release of Shadowfax *Live*, the tracks for which had been culled from special performances at now-defunct Palookaville in Santa Cruz, California, in January. The day prior to leaving, Chuck complained of soreness in his left shoulder and arm and of not feeling well, but he was insistent on making the trip. He was so looking forward to it. I assumed that the soreness was from his spending long days sitting at the consoles of our in-home studio as he composed the music for his album.

Still not feeling right, Chuck drove us to Ventura, where we spent Friday night with some longtime friends. Nine-year-old twins Gian and Greg accompanied us; our eldest son, Maceo, stayed behind because he didn't want to miss the first day of school. Chuck seemed to feel better Saturday morning and was upbeat and excited as we watched supplies being lifted by crane onto the Navy boat that would be taking us from Oxnard to Santa Cruz Island.

The seas became typically rough as we headed through the deep channel, but the ride was exhilarating as the wind hammered our faces, and pods of dolphins raced alongside us, jumping in the wake of the boat. Soon the peaks of Anacapa and Santa Cruz Islands loomed ahead.

Before long we had docked at Prisoner's Harbor, so named for its previous history as a place where inmates were incarcerated. By early afternoon we were ensconced at the ranch, watching with amusement as the twins played with the resident island fox, Josie. Although island foxes are endangered, Josie had been orphaned as a baby and rescued by the ranch staff. The twins would take turns chasing her around the ranch, and then she would chase them, nipping at their heels if they were too slow. They finally figured out how to outsmart her by one of them hiding behind a building, then the other running past the hiding place, exchanging places.

This way they never had to stop to catch a breath. Poor Josie was so confused by having two kids to keep track of she finally crawled off and curled up under a bush, exhausted.

I was raring to explore—in particular to return to Cascada, the natural waterfall two miles away that had been turned into a lovely, private swimming hole. Chuck, however, was feeling tired again and wanted to rest. So we spent the afternoon lounging by the pool and visiting with the caretakers, Dave and Debbie.

The ranch is in the central valley—Cañada del Medio—on Santa Cruz Island and is bounded on its southern edge by the Colorados: the Red Range. The stark, flat façades of the Colorados allow them to display their brilliance particularly at dusk, catching fire with the lengthening, late rays of the sun.

Constructed with adobe bricks and quoins shaped by Italian stonemasons, the Main Ranch House dates from the nineteenth century, having been remodeled in the Mediterranean style by the Justinian Caire family in the early 1900s. A front terrace facing a square garden is surrounded by a wrought-iron fence fashioned, along with all the balcony railings, in the island smithy. The house is at once elegant and comfortable—no wonder Chuck felt so relaxed here. It was like home only no telephones.

Gian [l] and Greg take a dip with Dad at Cascada, 1995

The next morning, Chuck seemed to perk up and we headed out with Dave in his patrol boat, checking the harbors to make sure that all visitors had the required permits to debark their boats, and also that there were no dogs on land.

In the afternoon Dave navigated us through coastal arches and caves—stygian in their damp darkness—while we explored the eastern coastline of the island. Cormorant-clad islets, whitened with guano, greeted us at each turn of the coast, and brown pelicans shared shore patrol. I took a long, deep breath of the clean, salt air, then smiled as I watched a V-wedge of these avian B-52s sail past our boat, the birds rising and falling, wings still but for an occasional flap, in synchronized flight paralleling the light rolls of the sea surface. At one point, Chuck commandeered the steering wheel and his trademark grin radiated like a beacon, reminding me how much he enjoyed boating. Then, he gave each twin a lesson in piloting. I commemorated their nine-year-old delight in my photos.

Knowing my interest in native cultures, Dave dropped me off at a rocky cove, armed with haphazard directions to an ancient midden. He couldn't land the boat because it was too rough, so he pulled up next to a large, relatively flat sunken boulder and I scrambled onto it, then up and around the cliffs. I never did find the midden, but I gained confidence in my ability as a mountain goat-cum-crab.

On Labor Day it was too windy to go out in the boat with Dave checking licenses, so we hung around the ranch playing with Josie and reading some of the books in our room. Most were very old: leftovers from when the Stanton family operated their working ranch. We had one of the cowboy bunkrooms with twin beds this time—funny for us because we had never slept in separate beds the entire fifteen years we had known each other. Chuck kept making jokes about how it was like the old Dick Van Dyke sitcom from the '60s.

Early in the afternoon we had Dave drop us off from the jeep at Cascada, where we enjoyed frolicking in the bracing water. Chuck played with the twins while they bobbed around and hung onto each side of him like human sandbags. I climbed over the cliffs and rocks attempting to get a good vantage point for picture taking, investigating the crow's nest in a dry basin above the deep pool in the rock wall bounding the fall, noticing the live-forevers sprouting incongruously from the cracks in the rock wall.

Live-forevers, stonecrops or chalk lettuce—common names for the genus dudleya—were a favored plant of mine, being one of the few succulents that I can successfully grow at home in Paradise Valley, where it gets too cold in the winter for most. I had cultivated a tiny native variety—of which there are forty in California—which I found sprouting on a large serpentinite boulder adjacent to No-name Creek.

* * *

Still not feeling well, Chuck decided to return to the ranch ahead of us to begin wild berry picking and a jamming session with our hostess Debbie, as promised. He had brought her samples of his plum jam which had just been awarded two blue ribbons at the Mid-State Fair: one for Best Plum and one for Best in the Men's Category. She, like everyone who tasted it, had gone nuts over Chuck's delectable fruit and wanted him to show her how to make it. Since the blackberry thickets around the ranch were in their prime of season, they decided to make jam.

We found Chuck and Debbie completely involved in jam production. Chuck was happy as a clam in his element. Part of jam making is the creation of a big mess, something ever appealing to him. By the time the twins and I arrived, he looked like a giant blackberry, covered head to toe in purple ooze.

Debbie proceeded to prepare a wonderful gourmet dinner, with Chuck providing the perfect complement: a bottle of wine brought with us in celebration.

Afterward, Chuck retired immediately to our room in the bunkhouse, complaining of indigestion. Since this was not unusual for him, I wasn't much concerned. I accompanied the twins to their room in the bunkhouse and began reading from *Señor Castillo, Cock of Santa Cruz Island*, a charming children's story written by one of the ranch's former residents, Helen Caire.

Upon returning to our room, I found Chuck reading a book he had discovered there called *Freaks* about the most notorious physically deformed people of the past century, including the original Siamese Twins, Chang and Eng Bunker. It was so fascinating that he got me reading it too. Eventually he began working on me to join him in his little twin bed.

At first I demurred. "No way! Not enough room! Besides, you're not feeling well and, I don't want to get sick."

But then he began commenting about how it was really turning him on being in twin beds, kind of like being in his mother's house with me as the "forbidden fruit" lying there so tantalizingly a few feet away. Eventually, what had not seemed at first a very exciting prospect developed into a highly erotic fantasy.

As usual, I couldn't resist Chuck's persuasive tactics. In a flash I had hopped into his bed and we were making love. Suddenly, he gasped—a deep, sucking, extended gasp—and became still, collapsing on me. I tried turning my head to see his face, but I couldn't. Not sure what to make of it, I thought he was joking at first.

"Come on, Chuck. Cut it out! This isn't funny," I said. I was pinned under him and tried wiggling to see his face and to move him off me. He was totally limp as I slid from underneath his still body. I tried to grab him to keep him from falling off the bed, but he was too heavy for me. He tumbled to the floor. Horrified, I realized something was terribly wrong.

His eyes were open and I looked into them, trying to determine what was going on. Listening for his breath, I realized with terror the awful truth—he had stopped breathing. I took his pulse and couldn't find one. I rolled him onto his back on the floor, trying not to panic and to remember my CPR training. I knew I had to blow into his mouth, but how long did I have to wait for him to exhale? And wasn't I supposed to check his air passage? But what could be blocking it when he hadn't had anything in his mouth? Should I be pushing on his chest instead?

I worked on him for about five or ten minutes, I don't know exactly how long—everything suddenly went into slow-motion warp and I lost all sense of time passing. I couldn't be sure I was doing the CPR correctly as all memories of previous instruction seemed to evaporate from my consciousness.

When I failed to get a response to the CPR, a complete and paralyzing panic set in. I didn't want to leave him but I knew I had to get help. Somehow I got myself over to Dave and Debbie's apartment and began banging on their door.

"Help—come quickly, Chuck's not breathing and I can't get his pulse!" I must have screamed, although I'm not how sure how much I conveyed aside from hysteria.

Debbie called the Coast Guard while Dave ran to our room to continue CPR. He worked on Chuck for an excruciating hour, taking turns with one of the ranch hands, all of us exhorting Chuck, "Come back! Don't leave us!"

During what seemed like an eons, reality began dawning on me. Chuck was not coming back. All I could do was sit there in helpless agony watching Dave attempt the impossible.

* * *

Finally, the Coast Guard arrived. As they loaded Chuck onto the gurney, then into the helicopter, I stood dazedly, hoping desperately to be wrong yet dreading the obvious, knowing I would never see him alive again. They wouldn't let me on the helicopter.

I never had another moment alone with him. Tears streaming, I could manage only to mouth goodbye, Chuck as the chopper lifted, hovered for a moment and slowly spiraled up the darkened valley and into the inky blackness beyond. I stared until its staccato rumbling no longer echoed from the Coronados.

The coroner who performed the autopsy said that Chuck would have been a candidate for quadruple bypass surgery, so clogged were his arteries. "Didn't you know all those symptoms—the soreness in his arm, tiredness, indigestion, cold feet—are classic for a heart attack?" the coroner asked, as if I weren't already feeling guilty enough.

Chuck's heart, so large in life, had failed him.

In that one instant my life changed irrevocably. I was now a widow. I began rolling the word around in my mouth, trying it on for size, despising it, choking on it, attempting to make it palatable nonetheless, hoping this was a bad dream, knowing it wasn't. The sense of personal annihilation defied verbalization. I'd heard it likened to losing a limb: a psychic limb. If only my psyche could grow back, like a lizard's tail.

But if there was one crumb of comfort in losing Chuck, it was in knowing that in death he did not suffer, and that he left our world doing what, after making music, he loved best. You could say he came and went simultaneously. And if, as the Tibetan Book of the Dead teaches, a man's last thoughts influence the condition of his reincarnation, Chuck must be on Cloud Ten.

XXI

THE
SECRET
OF
TIME

> Why is everybody left behind who is not dead in
> such a state of shock—as if this thing death, this
> losing forever of someone who has meant something
> to you has never happened before? Why is it so
> new?
>
> Jamaica Kincaid, *My Brother*

I am not a fan of funerals, especially those for people I don't like. So I was hard-pressed to understand how I came to find myself battling the congested freeways and smoke-filled skies of L.A. in order to arrive at Lesneski Mortuary in San Clemente one fall morning in 2003. But Stu Nevitt had called and asked me to be there, and I felt compelled to go, particularly after I discovered that no one else representing Shadowfax would be attending.

Stu's wife, Sheri, had died of an overdose of Valium, combined with alcohol. Although she didn't leave a note, Stu was convinced her death was intentional, prompted by a precipitous downward

195

spiraling in her life over the past few years. She had threatened suicide many times, he said, especially after he had filed for divorce recently. But he had not been swayed by her threats. He'd put up with her repugnant behavior far longer than anyone else, and he'd finally had enough. The only mystery was that Stu didn't leave Sheri years ago. But then, Chuck always said Stu was a "slave to fashion and accessories," and in Sheri he had found quite a package. It was an ornamented exterior that allowed him to overlook her many disturbing inner qualities, including her inability to handle alcohol.

But even when she wasn't drinking, Sheri was hard to take. After ten minutes of conversation with her, I would find myself wanting to get away. She was an insufferable know-it-all who, in fact, rarely knew what she was talking about, except when she found her niche in web design. Although this type of conceit often masks a person with low self-esteem, it was tough to feel sorry for Sheri because she made no attempt to change her ways or get help for her personality issues.

I guess I wasn't the only person who found Sheri distasteful. Of the few people who showed up to her funeral, none were her friends. She had too lengthy a history of luring and then betraying trust. Her only child from a previous marriage had been estranged from her for ten years because she had borrowed money from him and his father and reneged on repaying them.

One man who addressed the funeral attendees said he was her neighbor and "dog-runner." He spoke of how he had witnessed her "deterioration" of late, beginning with her involvement in an adulterous relationship with another man who found her a job as a website manager for a clothing manufacturer. When she was fired—she had never held any job very long, despite her skills—she retaliated by hacking into the website and deleting the files she had been hired to create. Her boyfriend then broke up with her

196

and she came running back to Stu, who agreed to attempt reconciliation.

Two days after she returned to Stu, the feds showed up at their door with a warrant for Sheri's computer, which they had traced as the source of the hacking. She was arraigned subsequently and charged with four felonies. Claiming they were cracking down on information technology crime, the DA let it be known he'd be seeking jail time, even after Sheri plea-bargained down to one felony. She responded by drinking. Stu said her alcoholism was worse than he'd ever revealed before: she became violent and abusive when drunk, which was why he had once again moved out of their condo and filed for divorce.

The last week of Sheri's life was one long alcoholic haze punctuated by hundreds of calls to Stu, begging him to come back. Stu said she left so many messages on his answering machine that it became overloaded and stopped recording. Then, on a Wednesday in mid-October, the calls stopped. By Friday, Stu became concerned, visited their condo and found her sprawled over the bed and floor, surrounded by little blue pills and empty vodka bottles. Her feet were the color of the pills.

Of course, none of these details were revealed at her funeral. Instead, a Christian minister—obviously hired for the event—delivered a standard eulogy laced with quotes from the Bible, despite the fact that he had been informed that Sheri was neither Christian nor religious. When Sheri's "dog-runner" spoke of her "Native American" spirituality, I noticed her mother glance quizzically at Sheri's father. This ethnic heritage was apparently news to them. But then, Sheri always did blur the line between fact and fiction.

So it was not surprising that Sheri's demise was under such tawdry circumstances. What did surprise me was my reaction at her funeral. I felt overcome by an inexplicable sadness. As the tears rolled down my cheeks, I found myself wondering why. I kept thinking about Chuck and feeling his absence, even though he'd been gone for eight years. Perhaps the sorrow we feel at someone's death is more for ourselves than the deceased. Perhaps grieving never really ends; it just accumulates until events like funerals allow its release.

* * *

As much as I dislike funerals, I like cemeteries even less. Let's face it. Cemeteries are creepy. After all, even if you can't see them, you know that they're there: dead people. Cadavers in various states of decay. Perhaps that's why they name them "Forest Lawn" and "Serenity Gardens"--designations that evoke tranquil settings, as if people really do go there to "rest in peace." Of course, we know that "resting" is not exactly what goes on in a cemetery, but the living—especially True Believers—seem to need these euphemisms for death. Instead of "dead," we prefer "passed on," "passed away," "deceased" or even "expired," as if we were talking about a grocery coupon.

Although my father was not such a believer, he expressed the wish to be buried in Rose Hills, a park-like cemetery that flanks the Whittier foothills in Southern California. An avid outdoorsman, John—as he asked us to call him—had settled with my mother, sister and me in suburban LA. because it afforded him the best year-round opportunities to hike and camp, his favorite pastimes. I think he wrote his wish for a cemetery burial into his will because he liked the idea of giving himself back to the mountains after all the years of pleasure they gave to him.

In fact, the mountains represented the essence of spirituality to him, and the few times I can remember his discussing religion were inspired while hiking. Once, when climbing Mt. Baldy in the nearby San Gabriel Mountains, we paused along the trail where the view through emerald peaks and canyons was particularly startling.

"Sights like these affirm my belief in God," he mused. "How could such perfection exist without the help of a Higher Being?"

I had no answer for this, and even if I had, I was too breathless from exertion to express it. I was twelve years old at the time and really hadn't thought much about or of God at that point. Our family had become lapsed Methodists after being asked by the local church to pay what John considered to be an exorbitant reinstatement fee following our return from a summertime vacation.

Mother stated little about her religious beliefs either, aside from taking my sister and me to church on Easter Sunday. Even this practice faded through the years. Ellie, as she asked us to call her upon our entering adulthood, had been raised a Methodist too, but this commonality was not enough to hold her marriage together. Not that Ellie didn't try. She continued to love my father until he died, insisting upon accompanying my sister and me to his burial. We stayed just long enough to watch the backhoe begin tearing up the damp, cold, January earth. Although initially I had not wanted her there, when the time arrived I was glad she had come after all. It would have been even creepier standing there with just my sister.

Although Ellie was sixty-two when she died, she was a perennial teenager at heart, partly because they surrounded her in her career as a high school English teacher. It was also because she had a youthful spirit, which perhaps influenced her decision to become a teacher in the first place. Ironically, though she related well to her students, I recall our relationship as being at its poorest when I was a teenager. Years later, I understood this antipathy to be caused—at least to some degree—by my father's subtle influence. Fortunately, owing to her limitless patience and tolerance, we were able to work things out and were getting along well when she died. This patience and tolerance gained her many friends, several of whom I suspected as taking inordinate advantage of her kindness. However, this never seemed to bother her. She was of a rare breed that always managed to uncover the best attributed in an individual—something that had little to do with any particular religious dictates. It was simply her way to accept everyone as they were.

Like John, Ellie made it clear what she wanted us to do with her body after death: cremation. However, she never mentioned what we should do with her cremains. At the time, in 1980, I was entering a transient phase of my life and hesitated to acquire more possessions. My sister had no interest in keeping Ellie's ashes either. Since Ellie had lived the last twenty-eight years of her life in Whittier, we considered Rose Hills once again. A check with the mortuary confirmed that she could, indeed be buried in the cemetery. In fact, there was enough space for her in John's plot, which was already paid for and would therefore save us the added expense of buying another one. We decided that this would be the perfect way to get our parents back together again, despite their divorce. I guess you could say we got the last laugh, although there might be hell to pay on Judgment Day. The image of my parents rising from their shared grave amuses me. I imagine my father glaring at my mother and saying, "What the hell are you doing here?"

* * *

As difficult as it was losing my mother and father, nothing—least of all my Ivy League education—prepared me for the death of my husband, Chuck. Perhaps this is because when I lost my parents, I had the luxury of retreating into total self-indulgence. Instead of seeking professional help, I self-therapized. But when

Chuck suffered his fatal heart attack, I had my three young sons to worry over. I couldn't run away or lose myself in a haze of drugs and alcohol as I'd done in the past.

I suppose that my grief will not fade until I am willing to release it and accept that Chuck is not wholly, irretrievably lost, even when I cease to remember him, or when his image no longer comes unbidden to my mind. But until then—and I cannot yet fathom the possibility of this eventuality—there is no escape from the intolerable sadness.

I distract myself from this reverie by contemplating how Chuck is still broadening my horizons, despite his physical absence. That's why I can't yet bring myself to clean out all his possessions from our bedroom, including the books and junk behind the headboard drawer. I keep thinking I'll want some treasure of his, or our sons will, or that there is solace in the mere physical presence of his things, even though I know that it is his intangible qualities that will endure long after Chuck and his material possessions are gone. In the meantime, I remain stuck between hanging on and letting go.

* * *

Chuck's memorial service was special in more ways than one. Our dear friends Ken and Tricia Volk offered to host it at their Templeton winery, Wild Horse—something that had never been done before or since. Mourners included our personal friends as well as music business people. There was even a collection of our sons' classmates in attendance.

My sister, Jill, sat next to me holding my hand as one by one several people stood up to speak. Bill Johnston had flown in from his home in Illinois and regaled the crowd with stories about how he'd first met Chuck in the third grade when they sat next to each other in the back of the class as a result of alphabetical assignment. Before long, the teacher realized they were not "back-of-the-class" kind of boys. As Bill spoke, I realized that being a "cut-up" was exactly what had initially attracted me to Chuck as well. And Chuck would have appreciated that Bill managed to make us laugh despite the sadness of the occasion.

We needed to laugh, too, for among those in attendance was one who had become estranged from Chuck in recent years. Although G.E., like me, was unable to speak, he wrote later that "Chuck's memorial was so necessary for me; it is hard to speak about. Chuck has brought us back together again, just as he brought us back together in 1982."

Those who were able to speak included a member of the neighborhood group that sued the city to halt quarrying at the Milhollin Mine down the road from us and told of Chuck's dedication to the group, our sons' Cub Scout pack leader, and the local rabbi. All mentioned the man who was like a second father to someone else's son. A man who was a caring and concerned neighbor. A man who loved children and loved to play. A man who knew how to have fun.

Phil Maggini, G.E. Stinson and Chuck [l-r]
in Illinois, 1972, courtesy of Bill Johnston

Chuck left no instructions about what to do with his body, except to say, "just do the easiest, cheapest, most practical thing." This, of course, meant cremation. But, as with my mother, the question became what to do with his ashes. I thought about sprinkling them around his beloved plum trees, whose fruit he turned into award winning jam years ago. I also thought about sprinkling them around the concrete park bench that a group of friends and neighbors had constructed and installed at Atascadero Lake in 1996. Inscribed upon a plaque that is centered on the bench back are the following words:

In Memory
CHUCK GREENBERG
1950 to 1995
Husband, Father,
Musician ... Our Friend

The bench is a fitting tribute to him, and I like the idea of celebrating Chuck's memory in a park—a far nicer place to visit than a cemetery. But I still can't bring myself to place his ashes there or anywhere else, for that matter. Instead, they remain in the same spot—the headboard of my bed—they've been since Phil picked them up at the Santa Barbara mortuary and brought them when he came to the memorial service we had for Chuck following his death. The ashes are inside a nondescript gray plastic box that was provided by the mortuary and is about the size of toaster, which in turn is inside a handmade straw box decorated with wide Polynesian-print ribbon and topped with a scallop shell, a gift that my sister picked up in Hawaii. Every so often I open the boxes and run my fingers through the silky, softness of their contents. I am somehow comforted by them.

* * *

I went hunting for the spare set of car keys one day. First, I dug through the drawer where I last remembered seeing them. No luck. I wracked my brain, wondering if I had "secured" them in such an obscure place that even I could not recall where. This had become an all too familiar situation for me: not remembering where I'd secreted various items. Becoming more and more frustrated, I looked into the headboard cabinet behind what was once Chuck's side of the bed--an area where he kept personal things like his Rolodex and wallet, which has remained pretty much intact since his death eight years ago. No keys surfaced, but I found several books, including his John Berryman collection. I became distracted from my initial key-seeking as I began perusing these books.

Chuck was always a diehard Berryman fan. In fact, an ideal date for him during our "courtship" was to hold me captive in bed, as he did on our first date, drinking sparkling wine, often Freixenet—which could be had for three bucks a bottle at Trader Joe's in those days—reciting, or forcing me to read, passages from *The Dream Songs*. Was it ever possible to just say no to Chuck during these times?

His friends often recalled how persuasive Chuck could be. G.E. remembered being in Chuck's apartment in Chicago with a bunch of his pals while he recited something from *The Dream Songs*, "all of us stoned out of our minds on pot, a common occurrence in those days," G.E. said. Chuck had ranted about how great Berryman was, going on and on and finally forced them, just as he did me on our first date, to listen while he read an excerpt. "I remember having the same experience I had with anything when I was high, total absorption and floating in the words like music," said G.E. "When he was finished, Chuck looked at us, waiting for a response, and Phil said something like, 'I don't know, it's too abstract. I like Bukowski better.'

"Of course, who knew if this were the truth or just an attempt to torture Chuck, which was one of the things that we often indulged in, like the evil adolescents that we were," said G.E. "I piped right in saying something that yanked Chuck's chain even more. Naturally, Chuck totally cooperated in the process, denigrating himself verbally and torturing himself physically by smashing beer cans on his forehead. It was one of the things that made Chuck such a lovable and infuriating person: He wasn't that serious about many things, even the stuff he was serious about."

And now, next to the bed a tattered *Dream Songs* resides still, along with *Recovery*. I recognized *Recovery* as a book I found for Chuck at a Cal Poly sale years ago when I was taking classes there.

Although I knew that the "recovery" to which Berryman referred was through the Twelve-Step AA Program, I wondered if there might be something of value in it for me, in what had become a rather lengthy recuperation from injuries sustained in a fall down some concrete stairs. And I also wondered if there was anything about grief recovery that related to alcoholism recovery. As I scanned the list, I kept getting stuck on Step Two: "I came to believe that a Power greater than we could restore us to sanity."

My agnosticism prevented me from acknowledging with any certainty "A Greater Power." If there was a Power, I did not perceive it to be "greater" than myself. If I were an alcoholic, would this revelation deem me untreatable? Is that why Berryman killed himself: loss of faith combined with the discovery that he was doomed to an interminable repetition of increasingly damaging binges? Was this lack of belief in "a Greater Power" what was prolonging my grief recovery? After eight years of Chuck's absence, there were still so many instances of abject misery. Too many instances. Not surprisingly, that day was one of them, for it was the anniversary of his death.

* * *

It has been years now, and Chuck still receives the most mail. It amazes me that merchandisers update their records so slowly. Although, ironically, the life insurance peddlers rank near the top of the most tenacious list, the worst offender is the bank. It has been sending statements to Chuck throughout the years he's been gone, and today I received a new credit card in his name. I have called them and written numerous times, beseeching them to change their records. They keep promising and failing. In fact, the rep who called recently asked for Chuck, even though my own name, not his, was very clearly written on the letter I had mailed. I, once again, had requested that they remove Chuck's name from their records in the same letter. I practically hung up on this bank guy because such requests for Chuck usually signal a telemarketer. When I'm in a perverse mood, I get satisfaction out of telling these solicitors, "I'd love to let you speak to Chuck. However, it will be a little difficult since I haven't been able to hook a phone line up to his ashes."

And so it astounds me how a dead person can seem more "alive" than a living being. Chuck certainly exists in reality for these moneymen. But I, apparently, died with him, as far as they're concerned. The guys in Shadowfax may have lost their careers when their band mate and leader died, but I lost my identity. I had no idea, until he was gone, how much my personal sense of self was tied to Chuck. When he died, it was as if a rug had been pulled out from beneath my feet, sending me catapulting through gravity-less space—a tether ball gone berserk—launched from its pole.

When I married Chuck, I became part of the "Chuck Greenberg Entity." And because that entity had celebrity status, another variable was factored into the social equation. I was always thrilled to bask in Chuck's limelight and live vicariously through his achievements. Unfortunately, when the Chuck Greenberg Entity lost Chuck, I became a nonentity.

Yet, I don't blame Chuck—I was an enthusiastic participant supporting him in his rise to fame, something he handled so well. Despite his celebrity, it never seemed to go to his head. His old friend Dick Howard said that Chuck's presence was always pretty much the same: "relaxed, accepting, open, always smiling, frequently with a sly undertone to that smile. Chuck handled his notoriety with such aplomb, really cool. I mean, he didn't change at all from that guy who used to show up at my basement parties where we'd all worry about whether anyone would give us a break during spin the bottle."

Thus in mortal life was Chuck schlepping us on an eternal adventure. He guides me still with his spiritual presence—in fact, he is a regular inhabitant of my dreams—of all our dreams, including the guys from Shadowfax.

Stu gets the feeling Chuck's "still watching out for me. One of the funniest dreams I had was one in which we were doing a Shadowfax record," he said. "Peter Gabriel and Eric Clapton showed up and were freaking out over the great drum part. Chuck had to tell him that it was a part Phil programmed on a drum machine. In real life Phil used to drive me crazy with his parts. We'd start with his drum machine part, then he'd make me go through every possible variation of it and would always go back to his original part—every time!"

In my dreams, Chuck has appeared long after we've become accustomed to his absence and has acted like nothing's unusual; he's merely returned from an extended road trip. I had a dream like this about my mother in 1982, soon after Chuck and I married. It seemed like she had "returned from the dead" as if she'd only been on some long vacation. As we conversed, I was thinking about how much I missed her and wanted to tell her so, but we were so engrossed in talking about other things that I never got a chance to. When I awoke it was as if in a fog, and I was momentarily disoriented. At the time, I attributed this disconcerting sensation to the first night spent in my sister's new home, which was where I had this dream, but after having had a similar dream about Chuck, I'm not so sure.

In other dreams about Chuck—like the one in which the two of us are inside a meat locker not unlike the one in the infamous Satriale's Restaurant in *The Sopranos*—I got the distinct feeling he was watching out for us. Chuck was telling me that he'd purchased all these carcasses hanging from the ceiling for me and our sons. I protested, saying, "But, Chuck, you don't even eat meat!"

"Yeah," he said in his mock Yiddish accent, "But I got such a deal." I awakened wondering if these carcasses—besides representing death—were somehow a metaphor for all the albums Chuck recorded and how delighted he was to be making royalties on compositions that were, in some cases, over twenty years old. It is money that I continue to receive, and has certainly been a boon for me and our sons, helping us to get through financial difficulties following his passing.

The night of the sixth anniversary of his death, I dreamt that Chuck kept calling and telling me to meet him at a specific place and time. I'd arrived at the designated spot only to wait what seemed like hours before finally giving up and walking home alone in the dark, making it all the more difficult to find my way. It was as if I'd forgotten where I lived; I was lost. And without Chuck, that's often how I've felt in my waking hours: lost; at a loss; a loser.

These dark, alone and lost images are not confined solely to my dreams about Chuck; I've had similar impressions in dreams about my father as well. In 1978, before I met Chuck and five years after my father died, I dreamt that he was living alone in a small house that was approached by entering a warehouse-like building and taking an elevator up one floor to what appeared to be the roof, although the elevator ascended inexplicably to higher floors. John's roof-cottage was surrounded by a small courtyard or garden with a fence around it. After hanging out with him for a while, I left alone to attend a staged show in a nearby theatre which involved the participation of some of the audience from the front row, including me. I noticed that all of us dancing wore black leotards and tights. After the show, I returned to the warehouse but could not remember where exactly my father's cottage was or how to get there. But I took the elevator, which was crowded now with people, and it occurred to me that his cottage number was "122." I remembered that I needed to get off on the second floor, but the elevator did not stop flush with the floor, and I had to crawl and hoist myself up to it, embarrassed by the less than graceful spectacle I was making. Finally, I managed to find the cottage and spotted my father in his garden-courtyard. The sky was cerulean, the sun was golden, and he was smiling as if eager to see me. He appeared gaunt as he had at the end of his life but not ill or infirm. We entered the cottage and I noticed it was very dark, with no windows. I sensed vague feelings of discomfort despite his good humor, but awoke grateful to have spent time with him, if only in my dreams.

Chuck inhabits our waking hours, too. Phil has regular conversations with him, especially when he's had a few drinks of the Crown Royal I send him for his and Chuck's birthday—as per Chuck in his will instructions. The birthday after Chuck's death Phil sent me a pencil portrait of Chuck playing a recorder. He is a young Chuck—one of the few times during his life that he wore contacts instead of his trademark spectacles. He's also a hirsute Chuck. I am reminded of the story about Chuck's dad calling him "The Hairy

Bastard" during this phase, and I laugh, a good sign that shows I can time travel down Memory Lane and not focus entirely on sadness.

Phil taped the following note to the back of the drawing: "This is the first birthday in 28 years that I've had to spend without my life's friend and brother. This drawing was a way to spend a few hours with Chuck. I sat out on the deck, poured us each a drink, and had a nice long talk with him." Phil let him know that we were all working on finding our balance.

Chuck playing the recorder, drawing by
Phil Maggini, 1996

G.E. finds his balance through the understanding that "in some way I will never really get over the loss of Chuck and our band. It's not possible for me to lose someone or something that means that much and not grieve for the loss of that person or that relationship. I think this will be an ongoing process." What has helped him most is looking into the question, "What is suffering?"

This is the question that fueled the Buddha in his search for an apprehension of his life and its circumstances. As Milarepa Lama said, "All worldly pursuits have but the one unavoidable and inevitable end, which is sorrow: Acquisitions end in dispersion; buildings, in destruction; meetings, in separation; births, in death." Obviously, life is filled with suffering and loss. It is what we make of that suffering and loss that determines the quality and value of our lives. In remembrance of Chuck's death, G. E. placed a picture of him on an altar in his bedroom and offered incense. This is his way of honoring him and reminding himself of how precious his life was and how precious our lives are.

* * *

And so Chuck has propelled me, however unwillingly, to embark upon yet another Wild Ride: Life Without Him. It helps to know that I am not alone in seeking contentment and fulfillment in my manless situation: many widows, divorcées and never-married women around the world have managed and even thrived in similar circumstances. I am heartened by Mary Austin's tale of a Shoshone woman: "A man," says Seyavi, "must have a woman, but a woman who has a child will do very well." In widowhood, "Seyavi learned the sufficiency of mother wit, and how much more easily one can do without a man than might at first be supposed."

Thus, I am learning the "sufficiency of mother wit" as well, as I embrace my manless parenthood. With our three sons perched to leave the nest, I face further change, being not the person I once was, nor yet the person I am to become. I accept this transience as another of philosopher Charles Taylor's maxims: "The issue of our condition can never be exhausted for us by what we are, because we are always also changing and becoming." My losses have rendered me opportunities for personal growth and transcendence. And, so long as I keep growing, I suppose I'm not dying. As Paul

Bowles once said, the journey of life "must continue—there is no oasis in which one can remain." It is a journey at once terrifying and liberating.

Chuck in 1991, by Marcia Wright and Doug Allen

* * *

CODA

One of My Blacker Days

Chuck Greenberg

It was one of my blacker days
with nothin going right.
I looked for inspiration
But there was none in sight.

So, I started drinking early
just tryin to get right
Some women look their best in bars
It must be lack of light.

I said if you'll come with me
I'll let you feel my pain.
She said I'll do the same for you
I'll even take the blame.

I knew I'd made a big mistake
But we were at her place
And as the clock ran down,
I felt like a clown,
I couldn't look her in the face

She had a mole, a dimple
An inserted nipple
And one breast was twice the size.
An abdominal scar,
That ran as far
As the heaven between her thighs.

APPENDICES

TRIBUTES

G.E. Stinson, guitarist, founding member of Shadowfax, 1995:

From the outside, Shadowfax's story probably seems fairly ordinary. A bunch of guys share a dream of creating music and "making it." They struggle together to make it happen. Over the years their shared struggle creates a bond between them. They survive a great deal of adversity. They become successful, but their creativity is derailed due to the pressures of being a successful touring and recording group. Success and money feed their egos and undermine lifelong friendships. Many of them become involved in drug and alcohol abuse. Internal strife develops. Communication breaks down. Some leave. Someone dies.

It may seem ordinary, but it was not ordinary for those of us who lived through it.

Even now, I am not sure Chuck was ever in complete control of the many things he "managed," but I have learned the utter necessity of chaos which was an everyday reality for Chuck. The chaos of being alive—and he was so very alive. This may be the greatest lesson that he has taught me, but he has also left me with an understanding of what really matters—friendship, humility, laughter, compassion, and community.

Of course, I knew the Chuck who knew how to have fun. In fact, of all my many memories of Chuck, the most persistent is his laughter, his easy smile, his genuine sense of humor. Through all the adversity, pain and despair, I will remember Chuck laughing, and I will miss that laughter. I will miss that crooked smile of his.

Chuck has been my family and friend. And no matter what may have happened between us, my love for him was not diminished. I know this is true because of how much sorrow I feel now that he is gone. Having written that and knowing it is true, I also know that in another sense he is not "gone." Whatever it was that animated Chuck will never end. The memories may grow cloudy, the music may fade, but he will always be here with us.

Alex de Grassi, guitarist, 1995:

I'm going to miss you Chuck. Like you always said, "We went to different schools together." I'm going to miss your round red-haired head and your whole round self. Whether it was playing music, getting crazy, or making jam, as Miles Davis would say, you were "all up in it." So keep going, Chuck! Wherever you are, go find us some more comedians, cooks, and musicians to make life worth living!

Glenn Morrison, musician and longtime friend, 1995:

I quit playing music for some years, all the while staying in touch with Chuck. He would always finish the conversation with, "When are you going to play again, you fool?" and eventually I listened to him and started playing again. All this time I was following the progress of Shadowfax. I was hugely proud of Chuck, Phil and Stu, of all of their accomplishments. A Grammy, ten CDs-- but I was proudest of their unwillingness to compromise their convictions as creative musicians, to play from the heart, to create their music, not mimic others. What an incredible virtue.

A couple of years ago, Chuck called me and wondered if I could play on their latest CD. Unbelievable—me on a Shadowfax CD. I will never be able to describe the thrill I had in being with those guys on that day/night in Los Angeles. Chuck knew how exciting it was for me, and he gave me that opportunity. He could have asked anybody, but he asked me because he knew what happiness it would bring. I wonder if he knew just how much happiness he gave to others. How fortunate I will be if I touch one individual the way Chuck has touched all of us. His laughter, love of life, and dedication to his art will be with us always.

1968 high school grad

Dru Markel-Bloom, friend, 1995:

Chuck was a wonderful human, an old soul, whose honesty, humor and loyalty I admire. I paint to his music and it has placed a charm over my studio. He was what he was, as honest as stainless steel, funny, kind, understanding. I have memories of his house in Crete, Illinois, overlooking a cornfield, and our upright piano in the corner (I will never know how he got it away from my mother) and Saturday night smoky jubilees, Chicago Heights style, at Luigi's. I remember shopping together at Army/Navy stores in Boston and his lectures on mucus-free dieting, which I must say were sweet, earnest and not a little bizarre. I remember his buying me cokes after Sunday School and his black and white photographs which were so lovely, so sentimental, even at thirteen.

He was the only person to call me my childhood nickname without a tease and as an adult. That name coming from his mouth first startled, then bathed me in nostalgia. How could anyone have feelings of nostalgia about Park Forest? It was a featureless place. But, when the wind blew around the corner of the building and bowed the grass, and fall was in the air, and we had cokes in our hands, all seemed right with the south suburbs. I felt his friendship and encouragement. I saw it in his eyes. He was going places. He was the bravest of us all.

Russ Davis, music programmer, 1995:

I first met Chuck about a decade ago when he and the other members of Shadowfax bounded into my radio control room in Atlanta. I already knew that their music was totally unique and I was soon to find out how equally unique the music makers were as well. Chuck did most of the talking, and with the gleam of a Christmas elf in his eye, he drew me into the magic of his musical dreams. In the almost twenty-five years of my radio career I have met and interviewed hundreds of artists. I can count on one hand the number whom I could call a true friend. Chuck was one of them.

I know he has left us far too early, but at least we can be sure that he has left us with so much more than most people ever dream of accomplishing. He was the most serious of composers and musicians, but never seemed to take himself or the work too seriously. He was an innovator with his groundbreaking work with the Lyricon and the hybrid of music he created fusing blues, jazz, rock and international influences, but at the same time he captured the essence of what it means to be a musician when he played. He was one person, one instrument, truly emoting.

If Chuck could tell us now what he loved the most about his life, it would be his family. His love for Joy and the boys is legendary. I never once spoke with him without his mentioning them. Word has it that my family was started in the room Chuck used as his personal home studio. It's a magical place, that house in Paradise Valley!

Chuck was a man with infinite creativity, and endless joy for life. A man with a perpetual smile on his face and a story to tell. He was also a friend anyone would want to have. Who else could give you a package filled with his own award-winning jam as a holiday gift? When I say Chuck was the kind of friend who would give you the shirt off his back, I mean it. I once admired a t-shirt from his radio station, K-Otter. He took it off and gave it to me on the spot!

The last time I saw Chuck was the summer of '94 when Shadowfax performed for CD 101.9's outdoor concert series in the plaza at the base of the twin towers of the World Trade Center. The band was marvelous that day. There were thousands of people there, some of whom were probably hearing Shadowfax for the first time. I looked in their faces as much as I watched Chuck. The crowd belonged to him and he knew it. The spirit created by the music was wonderful. That moment is the one I will choose to remember Chuck by.

I'm going to close now and go listen to "The Dreams of Children." I've played that song on the radio and had people call in tears, remarking on its beauty. I'm sure I will cry now too, but at the same time I will smile as I count myself among the lucky ones who were touched by one of the kindest, friendliest, most talented people in the world, one who has left me with such rich and wonderful gifts. Thank you, Chuck, your spirit lives on forever!

Randy Kaplan, fan and reviewer, 1995:

I must once again reiterate just how much Chuck's music meant to me. It is so much more than just audio stimulation—it is a completely engrossing assault on the senses. I could tell you about the first time I caught the band live at Hofstra University here on

Long Island—that was ten years ago—and my life has been changed ever since. Since, then, I have never missed a show in the NY area. Over the years Chuck and the rest of the group provided the soundtrack for my life (my parents can attest to this). From time to time, I used to love calling Chuck, to see what was happening and to hope that he would say that Shadowfax would be touring soon. He was great; he knew how much our conversations meant to me! To me, this was like having Paul McCartney's or John Lennon's phone number.

On tour last year the band played a tiny dinner theatre on the Hudson River in upstate NY. The place held only 40 people. Now naturally you know who was in the best seat. When the band came in Chuck said, "This is great! We feel like we are playing in Randy's living room!" I have turned so many people on to him through my reviews—we will all miss him terribly."

Brandon Bankston, Shadowfax Fan Club President, 1996:

I discovered Shadowfax when I was in the seventh grade. I did my homework with Shadowfax playing in the background throughout my high school career and haven't stopped that tradition now that I'm in college. Last summer I had an MRI done because of an auto wreck I had been in. I'm not ordinarily claustrophobic, but it can be a bit unnerving to be in a tube barely as wide as you while loud buzzes and clicks fire off six inches from your ear. I was able to stay totally relaxed (and even almost fall asleep) because they allowed me to bring my favorite tape to listen to while they did the ninety-minute scan. I brought Chuck's *From a Blue Planet* which I had just been given. From the first notes I was transported out of the sterile, loud MRI unit and into a peaceful dreamland. Chuck's music has an effect like no other, and I will be playing it for the rest of my life.

Mark Bernstein, childhood friend, 1995:

Chuck and I did not see each other that often, but when we did, there was always an instant and strong connection. And when for whatever reason I would count up those people that I cared for, trusted and felt pleased to share the planet with, Chuck's name and face and humor and resilience and somewhat rueful smile would come immediately to mind.

Frank Warren, music columnist, 1995:

Though we only had met and talked on a few occasions, Chuck always treated me with great kindness, always offering a reflection on my most recent columns. I met Chuck while at Big Music, where we sold some of his records. He came into the record store not like the well-known and highly acclaimed Grammy Award winner he was, but like the fun-loving "dad" I came to know him as.

Maceo, Gian, Chuck and Greg [l-r] at Disneyland, 1989

Chuck was as active with his family and community as he was with being at the forefront of popular jazz recordings. Chuck and his wife Joy brought their sons when they judged the Mardi Gras parade; and I most recently visited with Chuck when he attended the Harlem Globetrotters game at Cal Poly with his terrific boys. He often asked about local musicians, clubs, and trends, demonstrating his interest in the place he loved so dearly, the Central Coast.

Before launching another tour last year, Chuck brought the band into Big Music for an afternoon concert. The stunning musicianship was overshadowed only by the leader's warm humor and animated rapport with the customers. It struck me then: it was obvious that the man was far greater than even his most brilliant music. There is an aspect of Chuck that People Magazine and most casual listeners will never know. I guess what I am trying to say is that though his music will, of course, live on forever. I will always remember Chuck in my heart by his smile.

Sheila Densmore:
I have been a fan of Shadowfax's music for over ten years now and was deeply saddened when I learned of his passing. I first discovered Shadowfax through the video In Concert and became a die hard fan of their music the first time I heard it.

There will always be a special place in my heart for Shadowfax's music that words cannot explain. The music that Chuck and the others created went beyond music for me—it was an experience! The emotions and memories that their music created in me will be with me forever. I never had the opportunity to meet Chuck, but if I had I would have tried to say these things to him. Even though I never knew him personally I knew him through his music, and because he shared his music with the rest of us, I will always feel as though he was a friend.

Just so you know, today is my birthday and knowing that I was finally able to share my thoughts and feelings about Chuck's music with you is one of the best birthday presents I could receive!

Joel Nakamura, artist, 1995:
    I never had the pleasure of actually meeting Chuck. But in a way
I did through his music. I had the honor of visually interpreting
two of Shadowfax's albums, *Magic Theater* and *Live*. Chuck's music
touched me deeply, there is so much soul in it. I shall play
Shadowfax often so Chuck's soul and spirit may continue to live
through it.

Nancy Kulp, friend, 1995:
    I could write a book,
        but these are my special memories of that
        unique, one-in-a-million man,
        Chuck Greenberg.
            a musical genius, a pioneer,
            one of the great characters of the world,
            a good father and husband.

    I remember:
        how the emerging group Shadowfax were all such good
                friends to me, like brothers,
        in Illinois in the '70s
            Chuck, Stu, G.E., and Phil
            I loved them all in magic, eerie ways;
            they haunt me still.
            (isn't it a miracle to keep friends for over 20 years?)

    I was there when...
        this Grammy-winning group was just newly beginning,
        being created in a grand old farmhouse in the Midwestern
                corn fields called the Triple B Ranch.
        (Maybe dreams do sometimes come true.)
        Chuck lived for his dreams and music,

A true, dedicated artist.
   I often felt our human, humdrum, everyday life
   was too much,
   or not enough for him.

I remember:
   Chuck as an amazing Christmas tree one Halloween;
      we plugged in his lights and he was the
      Smash of the Party.
   Chuck, when he got his first apartment,
      inviting Curtis and me to celebrate with baloney
         sandwiches and champagne.
   Chuck, then later vegetarian, absolutely wrecking our kitchen,
      cooking an incredibly delicious meal.
   Chuck, who felt the magic of Kauai, Hawaii
      with many happy escapades to Paradise
      (and only he could express it in his own,
      inimitable, dramatic way singing Bali Hai to the green
         majestic mountains.)
   Chuck, who always made me laugh
      and be glad to be alive, what a gift.

I heard a jazzy blues song the other morning,
   a Keep on Truckin' song
   and I thought it would be a perfect way for Chuck to go out...
      a great celebration down the streets, New Orleans-style.
   (Imagine him now connecting and communing, with all the
         musical greats
      in all walks of music,
      who have gone before him,
         jamming in the Great Beyond!)

Ha! I like to think of myself as the #1 Shadowfax fan,
    and I always will be, you know...
    Their music is in my head and their pictures are all around;
    they are a part of me.

We mourn and grieve the loss of this incredible man,
    our dear, departed friend...
        too soon, too soon.

Chuck will live on in all of us,
    (especially Joy, Maceo, Greg, and Gian,
    who collectively are one of Chuck's greatest
    creations.)
    His vivid, vital spirit will never fade.

Chuck will live on in all of us,
And for this we are grateful.

* * *

SELECTED DISCOGRAPHY

PURE SHADOWFAX 2006
Sony/BMG

WINDHAM HILL/SANCTUARY 1996
Windham Hill

SHADOWFAX/LIVE** 1995
Sonic Images

SHADOWFAX/MAGIC THEATER** 1994
EarthBeat!/Warner Bros.

^SHADOWFAX/ESPERANTO** (Grammy Nominee) 1992
EarthBeat!/Warner Bros.

CHUCK GREENBERG/FROM A BLUE PLANET** 1991
Gold Castle

SHADOWFAX/WHAT GOES AROUND** 1991
Windham Hill

WINDHAM HILL, THE FIRST TEN YEARS** 1990
Windham Hill

^SHADOWFAX/THE ODD GET EVEN 1990
Private Music

WILLIAM ACKERMAN/IMAGINARY ROADS 1988
Windham Hill

^SHADOWFAX/FOLKSONGS FOR A NUCLEAR VILLAGE 1988
Capitol (Grammy Award Winner)

SHADOWFAX/TOO FAR TO WHISPER** 1986
Windham Hill

A WINTER'S SOLSTICE** 1985
Windham Hill (NRAA Gold Record)

SHADOWFAX/THE DREAMS OF CHILDREN** 1984
Windham Hill

^ROBIT HAIRMAN/RESIDENT ALIEN 1984
MCA

SHADOWFAX/SHADOWDANCE** 1983
Windham Hill

AN EVENING WITH WINDHAM HILL LIVE 1983
Windham Hill

WILLIAM ACKERMAN/PASSAGE 1983
Windham Hill

SHADOWFAX/SHADOWFAX** 1982
Windham Hill

ALEX DE GRASSI/CLOCKWORK 1981
Windham Hill

Recordings marked with ** denote those produced by Chuck Greenberg

Recordings marked with ^ denote out-of-print albums

SELECTED URLS

Shadowfax Sites:

http://www.geocities.com/BourbonStreet/Delta/4420/
(Brandon Bankston's Official Shadowfax Fan Club Site)

http://www.tandet.freeserve.co.uk/shadowfax.html (Shadowdance info)

Related Musicians:

http://www.williamackerman.com (Will Ackerman)

http://www.truart records.com (Armen Chakmakian)

http://www.degrassi.com (Alex de Grassi)

http://www.chuckgreenberg.com (Chuck Greenberg)

http://music.aol.com/artist/main.adp?artistid=2584 (Chuck Greenberg)

http://www.stunevitt.com (Stuart Nevitt)

http://lightbubble.com/bowed/szmad.htm (Jamii Szmadzinski)

http://www.humandrama.net (Jamii Szmadzinski)

http://www.yslas.com (Ray Yslas)

Joy Greenberg

Labels and Vendors:

http://www.amazon.com (sells *From A Blue Planet*)

http://www.music-index.com/index.html?main=Music-Shadowfax.html
(Music Index, sells Shadowfax CDs)

http://www.rhino.com (sells *Live* video)

http://http://www.sonicimages.com/shadowfax/
(Sonic Images, sells *Live* CD)

http://www.wbr.com (Warner Brothers, sells *Magic Theater*)

http://www.windham.com (Windham Hill Records)

General Resources:

http://www.allmusic.com/cg/x.dll

http://www.folklib.net/

http://www.ibiblio.org/emusic-l/info-docs-FAQs/wind-controllers-
FAQ.html#4.2 (lyricon info)

http://www.obsolete.com/120_years/machines/lyricon/
(lyricon, Bill Bernardi info)

Printed in the United States
89626LV00007B/170/A